THE EVERYTHING KIDS' Dinosaurs Book

Stomp, crash, and thrash through hours of
puzzles, games, and activities!

Kathi Wagner and Sheryl Racine

Adams Media

Avon, Massachusetts

Dedication
To the Renfelds and to our families, for understanding and surviving

EDITORIAL
Publishing Director: Gary M. Krebs
Associate Managing Editor: Laura M. Daly
Copy Chief: Brett Palana-Shanahan
Acquisitions Editor: Kate Burgo
Development Editor: Katie McDonough
Production Editors: Bridget Brace

PRODUCTION
Director of Manufacturing: Susan Beale
Associate Production Director: Michelle Roy Kelly
Series Designers: Colleen Cunningham, Erin Ring
Layout and Graphics: Argosy
Cover Layout: Paul Beatrice, Matt LeBlanc

An Everything® Series Book.
Everything® and everything.com® are registered trademarks of F+W Publications, Inc.

Published by Adams Media, an F+W Publications Company
57 Littlefield Street, Avon, MA 02322. U.S.A.
www.adamsmedia.com

ISBN: 1-59337-360-0
Printed in the United States of America.
J I H G F E D C B A

Library of Congress Cataloging-in-Publication Data
Wagner, Kathi.
The everything kids' dinosaurs book / Kathi Wagner and Sheryl Racine.
p.   cm.   — (An everything series book)
Includes bibliographical references.
ISBN 1-59337-360-0
1. Dinosaurs—Juvenile literature. [1. Dinosaurs.] I. Racine, Sheryl. II. Title. III. Series: Everything series.
QE861.5.W315   2005
567.9—dc22   2005011012

This publication is designed to provide accurate and authoritative information with regard to the subject matter covered. It is sold with the understanding that the publisher is not engaged in rendering legal, accounting, or other professional advice. If legal advice or other expert assistance is required, the services of a competent professional person should be sought.

—From a *Declaration of Principles* jointly adopted by a Committee of the American Bar Association and a Committee of Publishers and Associations

Many of the designations used by manufacturers and sellers to distinguish their products are claimed as trademarks. When those designations appear in this book and Adams Media was aware of a trademark claim, the designations have been printed with initial capital letters.

Cover illustrations by Dana Regan. Interior illustrations by Kurt Dolber. Puzzles by Beth L. Blair.

This book is available at quantity discounts for bulk purchases.
For information, call 1-800-872-5627.

See the entire Everything® series at *www.everything.com*.

Contents

Introduction

If you have ever wanted to go back in time, really way back in time, here is your opportunity! In *The Everything® Kids' Dinosaurs Book,* you'll travel back to a time when dinosaurs roamed the earth. Your destination: millions of years back in time to an earth unseen and untouched by humans. A place where you will experience the life of the dinosaurs firsthand, from the tiny Triassic dinosaurs to the terrifying Cretaceous creatures and everything else in between. You'll learn the difference between bird-hipped and lizard-hipped dinosaurs and where different dinosaurs liked to live. Maybe you want to find out how the dinosaurs got their names or why some dinosaurs were peaceful while others were terrifying. That's all in here too, along with plenty of crafts, recipes, experiments, activities, and games for everyone.

In this book, you can explore new places and create edible volcanoes, journey through Jurassic jungles and have relays, and, of course, see the untamed world through a dinosaur's eyes. This ancient world is filled with dozens of different dinosaurs, really weird mammals, and some other very strange creatures. Soon you'll be doing the limbo, making a seismograph, turning eggs into rubber, experimenting with your own environment, and trying the raft challenge. This fun-filled book will have you digging up answers, looking for lost clues, reconstructing skeletons, solving puzzles, excavating candy out of ice cream, and so much more! All you need are a few items from your present world and some help from your family and friends. The fun is all here, waiting inside for you. Are you ready for the journey of a lifetime? Well then, let's get started! All you have to do is turn the page.

Rebecca:
I lost my pet dinosaur.

Drew:
Why don't you put an ad
in the newspaper?

Rebecca:
What good would that do?
She can't read!
I lost my pet dinosaur.

What does a giant Tyrannosaurus eat?

Anything it wants!

Did the dinosaur take a bath?

Why, is there one missing?

Chapter 1
The World of the Dinosaur

No Proof

Chances are, you've seen a lot of different types of animals. But have you ever seen a dinosaur, even in a zoo? Of course not. The only dinosaurs we see today are in books, movies, or toy stores. So how do we know that the dinosaurs were ever really here? The only proof we have is in the form of fossilized bones or skeletons of these reptiles.

For years, people have been finding dinosaur bones and trying to figure out what the dinosaurs might have looked like and how they must have lived. We can only guess about some of these things, because we don't have any live dinosaurs to watch and study, and there were no people living at the time of the dinosaurs who could leave any records of what they saw. People today have at least been able to come up with a name for these creatures. The word *dinosaur* comes from the combination of two smaller Greek words meaning "terrible lizard."

Because there are so many unanswered questions about the life of the dinosaurs and their world, dinosaurs probably will always be one of the world's greatest mysteries. Some people have dedicated their lives to trying to find out more about the dinosaurs. The more they look, the more they find. New information and new types of dinosaurs are being dug up every day, which constantly makes us change the way we think about these reptiles of long ago.

Guessing Game

We guess about things every day. Doctors try to guess how tall you will be by measuring how tall

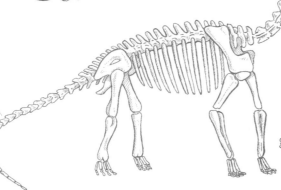

Who am I?

Once upon a time I had several names, one of which was Brontosaurus. I have also been called a "long neck" from time to time.

Who am I?

Apatosaurus

your parents are. Weather reporters try to guess what the weather will be. At parties, people are always trying to guess what is inside their presents. Scientists spend a great deal of time trying to guess when the next earthquake will happen. One of the hardest things for **paleontologists** is trying to guess what took place here on earth millions of years ago.

Your Turn to Guess

Guessing can be a lot of fun. If you want to challenge your friends or family to a guessing game, fill a clear container with several objects. Try things like beans, pennies, or small pieces of candy. Then show everyone your container, pass around a piece of paper and a pencil, and ask everyone to write down how many items they think are in the jar. If you want to make it a contest with a prize, you can give an award to whoever made the closest guess. If you want to guess too, have someone who's not guessing fill the jar for you. Another way to hold a guessing game is to guess who can limbo the lowest, jump the farthest, stare at each other the longest, and so on. How close was your guess?

No Man's Land

No humans were living at the beginning of the age of the dinosaurs 230 million years ago, and it's a good thing! You probably wouldn't have wanted to live at that time unless you happen to like sharing the neighborhood with crocodiles, lots of insects, and of course, dinosaurs! The dragonflies that were on Earth millions of years ago were ten times bigger than the ones that hover over today's pools of

Words to Know

paleontologist:
A paleontologist is someone who examines or studies fossils, like those of the dinosaurs. Paleontologists work in the scientific field called paleontology.

Fun Fact

A Dinosaur That Got Around
The Coelophysis dinosaur must have lived all over the big island also known as Pangaea, because its fossils have been found on every continent in the world.

What?

Begin by writing as many answers as you can under the clues. Then, enter each letter into its numbered box in the answer grid (one has been done for you). Continue working back and forth between the clues and the grid. When you are finished, you will have the answer to the following riddle:

What do you call a Nothosaurus with carrots in its ears?

Could you repeat that, please??

1F	2C	3E	4F	5D	6B	7F	8C		9E	10E	11F	
12A W	13C	14A N	15A T		16A –	17C		18D	19B	20B	'	21D
	22C	23D	24D	25B		26C	27E	28C			!	

A. Being identical

  T   W   I   N
 15 12 16 14

B. Water from the sky

 ___ ___ ___ ___
 25 19   6 20

C. Behaving badly

 ___ ___ ___ ___ ___ ___ ___
  2 13 28   8 22 17 26

D. To not play by the rules

 ___ ___ ___ ___ ___
 18   5 23 24 21

E. Round toy that goes up and down on a string

 ___ ___ ___ ___
  3 27   9 10

F. Popular fish in a can

 ___ ___ ___ ___
  4 11   7   1

4

water. These giant insects were the favorite food for the flying **pterosaurs**. And although dragonflies do bite, they were no match for a pterosaur.

In the day of the dinosaurs, there also were beetles, spiders, cockroaches, and eventually, snakes. Can you imagine what size these other creatures would have been if the dragonflies were that large? No one seems to know for sure when each of these creatures appeared or which dinosaur was the first. Scientists believe that the first dinosaur appeared in South America. Research also shows that the first dinosaur probably ate some type of meat, was about 3 feet tall, and ran on its back legs!

Words to Know

Pterosaurs:
Pterosaurs were bird-like reptiles that flew through the air during the time of the dinosaurs. Some of these pterosaurs had wings that spanned up to 40 feet across.

A Planet of Your Own

One way you can make a small version of the planet Earth is to make a terrarium. You will need a large clear container such as an aquarium or fish bowl, a handful of small, clean pebbles, a cup of charcoal or sand, and a small bag of potting soil. You should also have a few small fern or ivy plants, a small plastic cup or lid that you can fill with water, and a piece of plastic wrap large enough to cover the top of the container. Once you have all your materials ready, follow these steps:

1. Place the pebbles in the bottom of the container.
2. Follow with a layer of charcoal or sand.
3. Add enough potting soil to line the container about 2 inches deep.
4. Plant your ferns or ivy in this top layer and pat the soil down gently.
5. Place your plastic cup or lid in the center to form a pond.
6. Add some water to the pond and sprinkle a little around on your plants.

What do you call a dinosaur that left its armor out in the rain?

A Stegosau-rust!

Words to Know

fossils:
Fossils are formed when the remains of a plant or animal become replaced with sediment containing materials like sand that eventually hardens into stone, leaving an image of the plant or animal that once was

7. Cover your terrarium with the plastic wrap and set your new world near a windowsill, but not in direct sunlight.

Check your terrarium every few days to see what happens. If you watch carefully, you should be able to figure out how to take care of it. For instance, if it seems to be too hot in there, you can peel back some of the wrap or move the terrarium farther away from the sunshine. If it looks too dry, you may need to add a little more water.

Left Behind

When some of the dinosaurs died, their remains were preserved naturally or turned into **fossils.**

The dinosaur-studying scientists known as paleontologists have searched all over the world to find these dinosaur remains to help figure out what these wonderful creatures looked like. A great many of the dinosaur discoveries occurred by accident when someone happened upon a bone fossil while they were doing something else. Going camping would be a great way to search for dinosaur fossils.

A Camping Lifestyle

If you have ever gone camping, you probably have some idea of what a dinosaur's world was like, especially if you tried "roughing it" and sleeping out

under the stars! In the age of the dinosaurs, there were no houses, electricity, plumbing, or fast-food restaurants, which meant that there were no bedrooms or bathrooms, and certainly no cheeseburgers, pizza, or soda! The dinosaurs slept on the ground, ate whatever they could find, and had to brave the weather.

If you have ever been camping in a storm, you know how nice it is to get back to the safety and shelter of your own home. Although some of the many thousands of dinosaurs may have used caves for shelters, there would never have been enough caves to go around.

Pet Dinosaurs?

If humans had lived with the dinosaurs, do you think we would have dinosaur pets or dinosaur zoos? Would the dinosaurs have learned to like people-burgers? If dinosaurs had lived long enough, you might have been able to take dinosaur rides or go to dinosaur shows. There are quite a few animals that can be dangerous to humans today, such as tigers, lions, bears, and alligators. Many of them live in zoos or parks. Other animals that were dangerous long ago are now often people's pets. Even the first wild dogs and cats of the world were very dangerous.

The small dinosaurs may have been a lot like the small lizards we see in the world today. Some of these lizards make very good pets and are loved just as much as a dog or cat.

What's Your Age?

How old are you? If we didn't have records, how would you know? Sometimes older people aren't always sure of the date of their birth. A long time ago, not all babies were born in hospitals; many of them were born out in the country at

Who am I?

To some I probably looked like a furry elephant. I am famous for my long tusks and living in the Arctic regions thousands of years ago. Who am I?

Woolly Mammoth

Fun Fact

Billions of Years

Scientists believe that the earth is more than four billion years old. The dinosaur bones that have been found on earth are believed to be only millions of years old.

Words to Know

theory:
Many scientists have theories or ideas about the way that the dinosaurs used to live. One theory, or guess, some scientists have is that some dinosaurs had trunks like elephants.

their parents' house. You certainly can't always tell someone's age by their appearance. One guessing game you could try is to have your parents' friends try to guess your age. Then try to guess how old the people are in your family or at school.

Sometimes it's even harder to guess how old things like trees, houses, and furniture are. The first dinosaur bones really had to leave people wondering what they had found, especially if they only found part of the dinosaur! Dinosaur fossils can help a scientist support their **theory** about what happened in the past, and how long ago the dinosaurs lived.

The Big Island

Have you heard of the big island? Most people would probably think of the island of Hawaii. Many scientists believe that the earth is made up of many huge islands, much bigger than Hawaii, floating in a sea of lava buried many miles below the land and the ocean floor. Most of the land in these islands is buried underneath the ocean, but the part of land that is above the water looks a lot like a gigantic jigsaw puzzle. Scientists think at one time this "puzzle" was connected to form one enormous island. This big island is what was known as the ancient world, *Pangaea*. Over time, scientists say, the islands that once formed Pangaea turned and moved thousands of miles.

If you made a copy of a map of the world and cut out the continents, you could almost piece them together to form the original island. Or you can find a picture of the earth in a magazine and then cut it into puzzle pieces. How long does it take you to put it back together again? How long does it take your friends to do that? Can you name all of the continents that the "big island" eventually turned into?

If you want to see what Pangaea looked like before it split apart, you can look it up in an encyclopedia or on the Internet by typing in the words "continental drift" or "Pangaea." Knowing that the world is ever-changing, you could also draw a picture of what you think the world will look like in a few years from now or far into the future. Do you think it will end up as one big island again?

Holding It Together

As the islands or plates of the earth grow and move, the land is forever being forced apart. You can try holding it together the next time you and a few of your friends are in the pool. All you need are enough rafts so each of you has one. The idea of the game is to bring all of your rafts together to form one big island. Part of the group should hold the rafts together while each person, one by one, climbs up and

If at first . . .

Cross out each letter below that appears more than five times. Collect the remaining letters from left to right and top to bottom, and write them in the spaces. When you're finished, you'll have the answer to this riddle:

What do you call a dinosaur that never gives up?

T B R N B Y

B T R B Y N

T N R Y N C

E B R B A N

T O N P B S

_ _ _ _ - _ _ _ _ - _ _ _ _

_ _ _ _ _ _ _ _

I can do it!

9

Who am I?

Compared to other dinosaurs, I had a fairly large brain. I was a fast runner and I was a "true" mother to my babies when they hatched from their eggs (I took care of my babies). I was a smart hunter who liked to eat meat. Who am I?

Troodon

kneels on the island. Eventually, you should all be up on your knees holding hands and should be able to keep your rafts in the same area. If you don't get them all together at once, you're sure to have a good time trying. If you're determined to win, you might ask an adult to help steady all of the rafts until all of you are kneeling together on your island.

A Whole Lot of Moving, Shaking, and Bubbling

At the time of the dinosaurs, Earth was a fairly violent place full of volcanoes, earthquakes, and changes.

The dinosaurs had to find their way around the erupting volcanoes, through the bodies of water, and past the cracking and rising land. They were constantly on the move to find food, water, and shelter. Many scientists wonder whether the

Fossil Fractions

Look at the fraction below each blank. Pick the shape that shows that fraction, using these rules: the white part of each shape is empty; the shaded part of each shape is full. Write the letter of that shape on the line. When you are finished, you will have the answer to this riddle:

What do you call a fossil that doesn't ever want to work?

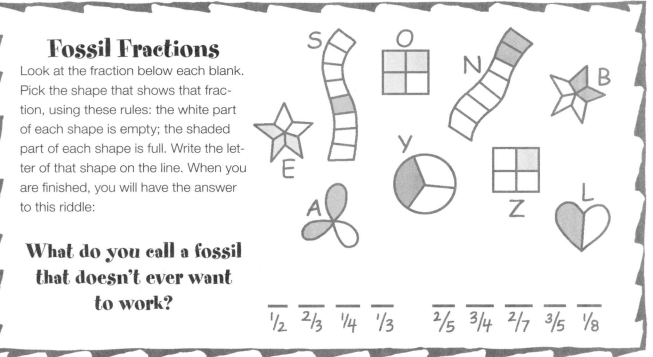

$$\overline{}\ \overline{}\ \overline{}\ \overline{}\qquad \overline{}\ \overline{}\ \overline{}\ \overline{}\ \overline{}$$
$$\frac{1}{2}\quad \frac{2}{3}\quad \frac{1}{4}\quad \frac{1}{3}\qquad \frac{2}{5}\quad \frac{3}{4}\quad \frac{2}{7}\quad \frac{3}{5}\quad \frac{1}{8}$$

dinosaurs were migrating as so many other animals do when the seasons change, or whether they just kept moving around to find new food.

A Tasty Volcano

Although the earth still has places that bubble and crack, they are fewer and farther in-between. If you want to see how the earth may have looked a million years ago, you can make this Volcanic Earth Cake. Here's how:

1. Ask an adult to help you bake your cake. You will first need to grease a 9" × 13" cake pan and preheat the oven to 350 degrees.
2. In a bowl, stir together 2 cups of flour, 3 tablespoons of cocoa, 4 teaspoons of baking powder, 1 teaspoon of salt, and 1½ cups of sugar.
3. Then add 5 tablespoons of softened butter, 1½ cups milk, and 2½ teaspoons of vanilla. Stir everything together.
4. Pour the batter into your greased cake pan.
5. Have the adult heat 2 cups of water in a pan on the stove. Add ½ cup of cocoa mixed with 2 cups of sugar to the water and stir until it is mixed well.
6. Pour this chocolaty liquid over the batter already in the pan and ask the adult to put it in the oven to bake for 40 minutes.
7. When the time is up, ask the adult to remove the cake from the oven. Then you'll need to wait a little longer to let it cool.

Try This

Earthquake Shake

When the earth starts to move, everything turns upside down. For fun, try this shake, which turns average ice cream into a sensation. With a parent's help, combine 2 cups of ice cream and ½ cup of milk in a blender. Put the lid on the container and then blend the ice cream and milk. When your shake is smooth, stir in a few crumbled cookies, chunks of a candy bar, some chocolate chips, or all three!

Try This

Fizzy Volcano

Here's a fizzy drink you can make that looks like a volcano that's erupting. Get a tall glass, and spoon in a couple of scoops of chocolate ice cream to make a mountain. Then scoop out a place in the top, for the hole in your volcano. To make your volcano erupt, pour in a little strawberry soda.

Fun Fact

Miles Apart

Did you ever wonder why only Australia has kangaroos, wombats, and the duckbilled platypus? Why Antarctica has penguins? Why there are so many places that don't have snakes? This is because the animal families were separated when the giant islands moved apart from each other.

If you want to have red lava on your cake, you can top it with canned cherry or strawberry pie filling after it cools. When it's ready, call your friends over and dig in!

Worlds Apart

Do you wonder if these big islands or continents are still moving today? Scientists believe that they are, but at a rate of less than an inch a year. They think it took hundreds of millions of years to create the big island and then it took about the same length of time for it to split apart to become the world as we know it today.

When there was one big island, the dinosaurs could have walked from one end of it to the other, so that members from the same families eventually could be found all over the island. As the worlds moved apart, some of dinosaurs weren't able to leave their home continent. Because of this, they developed in a variety of ways, as the dinosaurs in each area began to adapt to their changing environments.

What was the scariest dinosaur?

The Terror-dactyl!

Chapter 2

Sea Life

Try This

Look Mom, No Hands!

Can you touch the tip of your nose with your tongue? Can you touch your chin with it? Giraffes have really long tongues. A giraffe wraps its tongue around a branch and pulls off all of the leaves at one time. Some scientists believe that a group of dinosaurs called camptosaurids had the same type of tongue and probably did the same thing. Can you eat using only your tongue? Try one of these: pudding, gelatin, ice cream, grapes, or spaghetti.

Wonders of the Water

You might think that because the dinosaurs are gone, all of the animals that lived during that time have disappeared from the world. Actually, not all of them are gone.

From fossils that have been found, we know that some animal families have stayed the same for millions of years, never changing the entire time they've been living here on Earth. Coelacanths and the gingko trees can be described as "living fossils," because they are the only surviving species of a large class of organisms. No one is really sure why some animal families survive so long without changing. Sturgeons, sponges, horseshoe crabs, lobsters, lungfish, crocodiles, turtles, jellyfish, and sharks have changed very little or not at all.

How Big Was It?

Before the dinosaurs appeared, there were many other strange creatures living in and out of the water. There were even some reptiles that weren't dinosaurs, such as the Plesiosaur. Fortunately this giant marine creature never became a living fossil. Can you imagine if you were swimming along in the ocean, and suddenly what appeared to be a huge turtle without a shell raised its head up out of the water to take a breath of air and then headed right for you? If that wouldn't be scary enough, his big brother, the Liopleurodon, was usually trailing right behind

him! Liopleurodon was an enormous water creature that scientists thought possibly weighed more than any of the largest whales. Its teeth measured up to a foot long and its head was the size of a small car.

Grow Your Own Coral

If you want to make something that looks like coral growing in the ocean, all you need to do is find two disposable aluminum pie tins and gather the following ingredients:

charcoal briquettes
laundry bluing
water
salt
ammonia
food coloring

Next, ask an adult to help you with these steps:

1. Place a few charcoal briquettes, broken into small pieces, into the first pie tin.
2. In the second pie tin, mix 5 tablespoons of laundry bluing and 1 tablespoon of water.
3. Add 5 tablespoons of salt and mix well.
4. Ask the adult to gently add 3 teaspoons of ammonia to the mixture, stir well, and pour it over the charcoal briquettes.
5. If you want to color your coral, you might also want to add a drop or two of food coloring on it. Add the drops together if you want to create a mixed color.

From time to time, check on your changing coral. What do you see?

Words to Know

extinct:
When an animal becomes extinct, it no longer exists or lives on our planet anymore. Dinosaurs, along with many other animals, have become extinct or have vanished from our planet. Some animals are considered endangered, which means they are at risk of becoming extinct.

Which One?

I was one of the first real creatures on Earth millions of years ago. I looked sort of like a combination between a bug and a crab. My name sounds like I would be easy to lift, but some of us were fairly large. Which one am I?

   A. Long-legged Llama
   B. Haast's Eagle
   C. Trilobite
   D. Sea Mink

C. Trilobite

Who am I?

You may think I would go very well with pepper. I was one of the last of my kind to survive. For protection, I had both small and large bumpy scales inside the skin all over my back. **Who am I?**

Saltasaurus

Why do dinosaurs eat raw meat?

Because they don't know how to cook!

You Ate What?

If the dinosaurs ever had lived in the ocean, they would have had to eat the same things that other ocean dwellers ate, such as plants, fish, or other sea animals. People have also been known to eat things that come from the ocean. Maybe you have tried octopus, shrimp, or tuna. You might think a jellyfish sounds good to eat, but because jellyfish can sting, that would probably not be a good idea. But what if you could make your own jellyfish feast? You could even hold a jellyfish-eating contest! To make your edible fake jellyfish, ask an adult to mix up a few packages of flavored gelatin for you, using several flavors and the really thick gelatin recipe. After the gelatin is ready, cut it into a bunch of long strings, so that it looks like jellyfish tentacles. Mix and match your flavors, then divide up the tentacles between the players and see who can finish theirs first! If you want to make a whole fake jellyfish, make a separate big bowl of gelatin before it sets completely and place a few of the tentacles in the gelatin and over the bowl's edge. You and your friends can make it wiggle around and then serve it for dessert.

A Pack of Travelers

When the remains of dinosaurs are found, it often appears that they traveled together in groups. Many other types of animals tend to be found in groups, too. Can you think of any? Here are some examples: fish swim in schools, dogs run in packs, and lemmings even make mass migrations to jump off cliffs. However, today's reptiles usually live alone. Alligators are one of the few reptiles that remain with their young.

Shell Game

Many soft-bodied creatures that used to live in the ancient seas evolved into creatures with hard shells. These shells were good for two reasons: they gave the sea creatures much more protection, and they turned into excellent fossils! Find your way through this fossil shell maze from START to END.

Have you ever tried playing follow the leader in the water? In the shallower water, you and a few of your friends can follow the leader. As you go along, the leader can start trying different things for the rest of you to follow, such as standing on one foot, floating on your back, splashing the person behind you, and so on.

Tug of Water?

Another game you can play in the water is dinosaur tug-of-war. Try to mix and match the size of the "dinosaurs" on each team, so that the game isn't over too quickly. For this game, you will need two teams and a soft, cotton rope about 15 feet long. Tie two bandannas on the rope, each one about 5½ feet from each end. Then you will need someone to stand off to the side to be your judge. Once you are all standing in the water, which should be no deeper than about waist high, everyone takes ahold of the rope and pulls until one team's bandanna crosses the center area where the judge is standing.

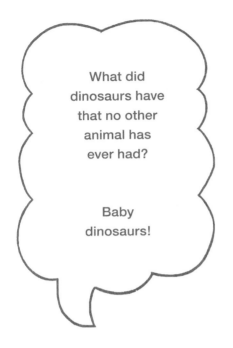

What did dinosaurs have that no other animal has ever had?

Baby dinosaurs!

Big Changes

Although we like to guess how the dinosaurs got to be the way they were, no one is really certain. Some people believe all living things may have started out in the ocean and then decided to come ashore. Others think they developed or changed from animals that were on the land. Before there were dinosaurs, there were many other creatures on our planet. They were strange creatures with strange names and strange bodies, such as the Eryops, Gerrothorax, and the Diplocaulus. All three had very short bodies, legs, and tails. Most scientists believe that some of the creatures in the sea evolved into **amphibians**, and some also think that some of the amphibians eventually evolved into reptiles.

Why didn't all the fish, amphibians, and reptiles evolve, and why did some of them become extinct? No one knows. Maybe someday you'll be the one to discover the answers to these questions.

Try It On for Size

Turtles and snails are among the other animals that like both the water and the land. It would seem strange to live in a shell all of your life. If you want to see what it would be like, you could try making a shell for yourself. All you need is a cardboard box that is a little bit bigger than you are, some glue, markers, and a few things to decorate your shell, like colored pieces of paper, stickers, or streamers. Once you have a box, ask an adult to help you make a door so you can go in and out easily. Next, decorate your shell with markers. Use several colors. To finish decorating your shell, stick the scraps of colored paper, stickers, or a few pictures on the outside of the box.

Words to Know

amphibian:
An amphibian is an animal that lays its eggs in the water. Most amphibians, like frogs, can live both on land and in the water. Amphibians are cold-blooded animals that have a backbone and rubbery skin.

Try This

Making a Big Impression

If you want to make some really big decorations for your room or your door, you can trace a picture of a dinosaur, cut it out, and lay it on an overhead projector. Then trace the larger dinosaur outline onto a piece of poster board or cloth to make your own dinosaur poster or flag.

Chop It Up

A riddle and its answer were put into the large grid, and then cut into eight pieces. See if you can figure out where each piece goes, and write the letters in their proper places. When you have filled the grid in correctly, you will be able to read the puzzle from left to right, and top to bottom. HINT: The black boxes stand for the spaces between words. Some pieces are turned!

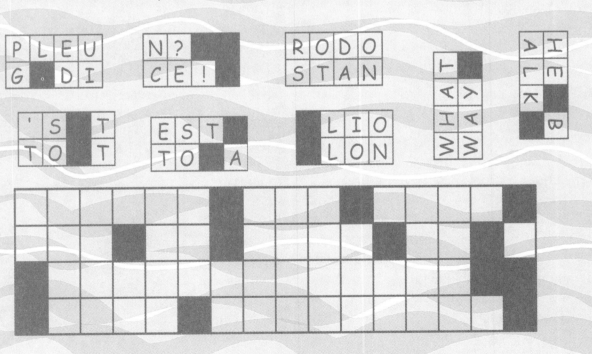

Once you're finished, you can try moving around with your new shell on your back. If you can find some friends who want to make their own shells with you, you could have a race to see who can move fastest inside his or her shell. The more people you can find to enter your race, the better. How does it feel to move around while carrying a shell? It's no wonder animals with shells move more slowly than the rest of us! One type of dinosaur known as an Anklosaurus probably found it just as difficult to travel as you did!

Coming Ashore

Most scientists believe that all life began in the ocean, but some of the creatures were not destined to remain in their watery home. Did you know that a fish called the lungfish is able to use its fins to walk on land? If the water where it makes its home dries up, it comes ashore and may spend months or years buried in mud until it rains. Scientists think that the amphibians evolved from a similar fish. As their fins gradually changed into legs, they became the first animals to live only part of their lives in the water. They were born with gills like the fishes, but eventually developed lungs, so that they were able to take in oxygen even after they had left the water. The only time today's amphibians have to return to the water is to lay their eggs.

Have you ever seen an amphibian? You may not think so, but if you have ever gone to a bait store and bought a salamander, caught tiny frogs as they tried to leap back into a pond, or found a toad hiding in the moist dirt in your garden, you have seen one. Although a few of the first amphibians were very small, many of them were bigger than a large dog!

Fun Fact

Something's Missing!

No matter how hard the dinosaur hunters have tried, no one has been able to find a complete Tyrannosaurus rex skeleton. They have found enough bones to give us a good idea of what T. rex was like, but they were not all found in the same place.

Who am I?

Putting my skeleton together again would surely take a long time. My body was sometimes stretched out over 80 feet long, all the way from the tip of my tiny head to the end of my skinny tail.

Who am I?

Diplodocus

Words to Know

reptile:

A reptile is a cold-blooded animal that usually lays eggs and has a backbone. Most reptiles have a scaly or tough skin. The dinosaurs that lived millions of years ago were reptiles. Snakes, lizards, crocodiles, and turtles are a few other reptiles.

These amphibians lived in a damp land that was covered with trees and ferns. Over millions of years, the plants on that land turned into the coal that provides much of our electricity today. In some places in the world, people still burn peat, a plant mixture that someday will turn into coal.

Reptile or Amphibian?

When scientists first discovered the fossils of the lizard-like animal they named Seymouria, they couldn't decide what it was. They were puzzled because it had a lateral line, which is a horizontal line on the side of the body that only amphibians and fish have. The lateral line helps the amphibians and fish find their food in the water. But if it was a water creature, why didn't it have webbed feet and why did it have teeth and claws? Eventually, they decided that this new kind of animal that looked like a **reptile** was actually an amphibian.

To Swim or Not to Swim?

The amphibians needed to enter the water to lay their eggs, but when they began to evolve they started to lay their tough eggs in nests away from the beach like reptiles do. Most of the reptiles had a rough skin that kept them from drying out as they made their home on the land.

If someone asked you to name a reptile that lives in the world today, you might say a lizard, a turtle, or a snake. If so, you would be right. Millions of years ago, reptiles came in all shapes and sizes. The Ichthyosaurus looked like a fish, but it wasn't a fish because it had to come to the top of the water to breathe. Numerous fossils have been found that prove

that this creature's young were born live underwater! For many years, scientists believed that Ichthyosaurus developed legs, came out of the water, then returned to the water, and developed fins again. They no longer believe that this is true. Modern scientists believe that Ichthyosaurus did not have any legs and spent its life in the water.

Warm-Blooded Versus Cold-Blooded

At one time, all reptiles, including the dinosaurs, were thought to be cold-blooded, which meant that their bodies were the same temperature as their surroundings. That is why you see modern-day reptiles like crocodiles, alligators, snakes, turtles, and geckos (which are all cold-blooded) sunning themselves on warm rocks and logs in the water. Today scientists are more puzzled than ever because they are finding fossils that appear to show that the warm-blooded birds' **ancestors** were the dinosaurs. A warm-blooded animal's body stays warm even if it is cold outside. A cold-blooded animal's body grows colder as the temperature drops.

There are still both cold-blooded reptiles and warm-blooded birds today. Were some of the dinosaurs warm-blooded and some of them cold-blooded? Even the experts don't know for sure! Some mammal-like reptiles that came to be known as cynodonts even had hair on their skin and were believed to be **warm-blooded**, just as you are!

Fun Fact

Fuzzy Dinosaurs?
When you think of dinosaurs, you probably think of reptiles with scaly skin like a snake or lizard. Did you know some dinosaurs' skin may have been covered in fur, feathers, hair, spikes, or plates?

 23

Words to Know

ancestors:

Ancestors are the people or animals in a family that were born before this generation. You descended from your grandparents and great-grandparents, so they would be your ancestors. The dinosaurs were ancestors of the modern-day reptiles.

Which One?

A smaller flightless bird, I became extinct only in the last couple of hundred years. Although there were many "great" things about me, no one really realized it until I was gone. Which one am I?

A. Heath Hen
B. Great Auk
C. Hawaiian Rail
D. Carolina Parakeet

B. Great Auk

Reptile Roundup

After it gets dark some night, gather a few friends together (with everyone's parents' permission) and tell them all to bring little flashlights. Tell them that you are playing a new game of hide-and-seek the way that snakes do. Snakes find their victims by sensing the heat from their bodies. In your case, you will be sensing the light from your friends' flashlights. Have the "snake" cover his eyes and count to 100. All the other players—the snake's "lunch"—must hide, and when the snake calls out "ready," they need to flash their lights one time, quickly, and then wait to see if they are found as the "snake" searches for the places where he saw the light flash. Each time the snake calls out, "Where's my lunch?" the other players must flash their lights again. The first one found is the loser, and he or she becomes the new "snake."

How Old Am I?

Dinosaurs aren't the only things that scientists study. Did you know that turtles have the longest lifespan of all of the animals and that their species has been on the earth longer than any other reptile that is alive today? One way to figure out the age of a turtle is to count the rings on its shell. But how do we know how old some of the dinosaurs were? Many people believe that the dinosaurs lived to be more than 100 years old. Scientists have found some clues in fossils that lead them to believe this. For one thing, they think that some dinosaurs may have been unable to move their tails as they reached such old ages, because their fossils show that their joints were filled with hard tissue. Other animals today have this same condition when they become quite old.

Scientists have also noticed worn places in the fossils of the dinosaurs caused by the dinosaurs' muscles moving back

There, There, It's OK

Use the numbered clues to fill in the bubbles. The last letter of one word is the first letter of the next. When you are finished, write the letters from the shaded bubbles on the dotted lines to get the answer to this riddle:

What should you do if you find a blue Ichthyosaur?

1. To grab a moving thing
2. Opening through something
3. A line where something ends
4. One of what you hear with
5. Hurry
6. Damp
7. Not bright
8. List of foods you can order
9. You and me
10. Drink little by little

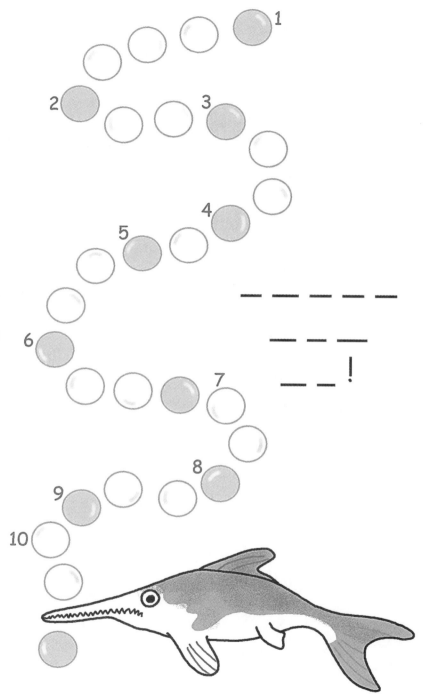

_ _ _ _

_ _ _ _

_ _ !

and forth across their bones for so many years. Learning the age of a dinosaur can be very important to a scientist. Many times the scientists have thought that they had discovered a new species of dinosaur, until someone else realized it was actually a baby or a smaller form of an already-discovered species.

Veterinarians can easily determine the age of a horse by looking at its teeth—all they have to do is see how worn down they are. Unfortunately, this easy method can't be used on dinosaur fossils. Many of the dinosaurs had several sets of teeth that were waiting in their jaws to replace the ones they lost. With these constantly changing teeth, you certainly wouldn't be able to look at their teeth to judge how old they were!

Fun Fact

Talented Tails

Dinosaurs used their tails like a leg to balance, as a weapon to protect themselves, and more. Although humans have a tailbone, we don't have a tail. Can you use other parts of your body in different ways? Have you ever tried using your toes to pick something up? How about painting or drawing with your feet? Another thing you could try is game of catch with a friend using only your feet.

Charlie: Why did the Triceratops cross the road?

Jesse: He didn't, the chicken crossed the road.

Charlie: Well, why did the chicken cross the road?

Jesse: To get away from the Triceratops!

Chapter 3

Triassic Times

Words to Know

expedition:
When the first dinosaur hunters went to search for dinosaur bones they called the hunt or journey an expedition. Some expeditions still take place every year.

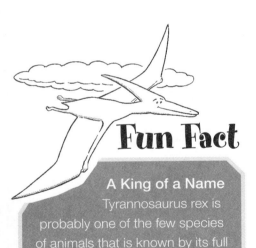

Fun Fact

A King of a Name
Tyrannosaurus rex is probably one of the few species of animals that is known by its full scientific name. *Tyranno* means "tyrant" and *saurus* means "lizard." *Rex* means "king."

What's in a Name?

Figuring out the names of dinosaurs can become a problem. The finders of the fossils try to use names that describe what they have found, but the scientific names are usually in Greek and mean very little to anyone except the scientists. Tyrannosaurus rex seems to be one of the few easily recognized scientific names. Other names come from the places where the fossils were found, those who found them, the people who paid for the **expeditions**, or the names of gods, soldiers, and myths.

If you found a dinosaur, what would you name it? Would you name it after yourself, as some of the paleontologists did? The Drinker dinosaur, for example, was named after a paleontologist named Edward Drinker Cope. If you used your last name and added the word *saurus*, what would the name of your dinosaur be? Maybe you would name it after its behavior, like the Tyrannosaurus, whose name means "tyrant lizard." Or you might name it for one of its features, like the Triceratops, which had three horns. *Tri* means "three," and the rest of the name comes from Greek words that mean "horn" and "face."

You could invent your own dinosaur by gathering several pictures of different dinosaurs and cutting them in half. What would your new dinosaur be called if you matched the front of one dinosaur to the back of another? How about a

Tricerasaurus rex or a Brontoceratops? Can your family or friends guess what your new dinosaur is? Now it's their turn to match the dinosaur halves and make up a few new dinosaurs of their own.

What's Your Name?

Where does your name come from? You can learn a lot about your family's history by researching a family name. Some people put their last names on their clothing, like basketball players do. Others put their names on their houses or the door to their bedrooms.

First names also can have special meanings attached to them. There are many books that list children's names and their meanings. Do you know what your name means? Some people wait to name their children until something significant happens in the child's life. Can you think of a name that your parents might have called you if they did this?

Who's Who?

How could scientists have been so sure that a dinosaur found in England was from the same family of animals as others that were found hundreds of miles away in a Belgian coal mine? How do they know that the part of a jaw of a dinosaur found in Mongolia doesn't belong in the mouth of a dinosaur from Argentina? Every living plant and animal in the world is given a descriptive classification and a very long official name, so that every scientist will know exactly what organism other scientists are talking about. Your scientific name would tell scientists that you are an animal with a backbone, which walks upright, has a thumb, and is an intelligent human being. *Homo sapiens* is the name given to humans. Just like humans, dinosaurs come in all shapes and

What made the dinosaur's car stop?

A flat Tire-annosaurus!

Try This

Family Flag

See if you can find out what your last name means. You might be able to look it up in a book or on the Internet. You also can look up the country where your ancestors lived. You may be able to find the country's flag or things like national flowers or other symbols. Make a family flag that shows some of this information. You could also make your own personal flag with the meaning of your first name.

 29

Ptiny Pterosaurs

Some of the smallest pterosaurs were so lightweight that they had to be careful to keep their wings folded when they were resting. Otherwise, the wind could blow them right off their perch! Can you help this pterosaur catch a dragonfly for dinner?

sizes, but they are sorted in a similar way. There are hundreds of varieties of families, and more are being discovered every year. Each time a new one is found, scientists give it an original name and map the location where they found it.

Lizard Legs

For years the dinosaurs have been named for their features or by the family that they came from. One of the earliest dinosaurs, Coelophysis, was a member of the saurischian branch of the dinosaur family tree. *Saurischian* means "lizard hipped," and *Coelophysis* means "hollow form." This dinosaur was as tall as a one-story house, but only weighed as much as a large dog. It ate insects, an occasional dinosaur egg, and maybe other Coelophysis.

The earliest amphibians couldn't move very quickly because their legs were short, they moved one foot at a time, and they squirmed across the ground. The reptiles' bodies were lifted up, the legs were closer to their bodies, and they could sprint short distances just like today's alligators and crocodiles. You might find that you could move pretty fast too, if you thought that they were chasing you! Over a long time, the reptiles' legs changed and slowly moved so that finally their legs were directly below their bodies.

When this happened, some of them learned to run using only their back legs. Many

Which One?

When I was alive, I looked like a cross between a zebra and a horse. I have been extinct now for a little more than a hundred years. Which one am I?

A. Quagga
B. Blue Antelope
C. Eastern Elk
D. Lesser Bilby

A. Quagga

Fun Fact

The Tail End

Did you know that some lizards' tails fall off when someone grabs ahold of them? This helps them to escape when a person or animal tries to catch them by their tail. These lizards have also been known to grow a new tail. Do you think some of the dinosaurs may have lost and regrown their tails too?

Who am I?

When you hear my name you might think I was named for part of your leg. You might know me by the triangle-shaped spikes and horns that were all over my body, or by the club-shaped end of my tail.

Who am I?

Ankylosaurus

of the early fossil hunters believed that some of the dinosaurs hopped around like kangaroos.

Crocodile Crawl

Have you ever tried crawling on the floor on your hands and knees like a crocodile? It's easy! All you have to do is spread your legs and arms as far apart as you can and try to crawl. Isn't it hard to move fast? It's also really hard to remember which arm or leg to move next. Now, bring your arms and legs in just a little and crawl around some more. Finally, bring your arms and legs directly under your body and crawl as fast as you can! Set up some races with your friends. To show how lucky you are that humans learned to walk in another way, stand upright and then race one more time.

What Kind of Lizard Is That?

Another member of the lizard-hipped dinosaur family was the Plateosaurus. He looked like a shorter version of the lovable long-necked dinosaurs that you see plucking leaves from the tops of trees in today's dinosaur movies. Although he weighed as much as two cows, he was pretty small in comparison to some of his descendants. Some scientists believe he would also eat meat at times and had claws like the true meat-eaters. The type of dinosaur most people would never want to know, the really huge meat-eater, didn't appear until much later, after the start of what scientists call the Jurassic Period.

The Hands Are Pretty Handy

The original dinosaurs' front legs, or forelimbs, as they are also sometimes called, had five fingers. By the end of the

age of the dinosaurs, many of them had only two fingers. Until dinosaurs starting using their front legs as arms to help them get their food, they had to reach out with their mouths and hope that their food would wind up in it. They couldn't even use their feet!

Have you ever tried using only your mouth to eat? Ask an adult to place things like French fries, potato chips, ravioli, or other small foods on several plates for you and your friends. Or they could dangle a cluster of grapes in front of you. Then try using only your mouth to grab your food. If you have just taken a bath, you could even try eating with your toes!

Bird Legs

Have you ever noticed how much a dinosaur looks like a great big bird? Apparently, the scientists who named certain types of fossils thought so, too. Besides the saurischian, or lizard-hipped, branch of the dinosaur family tree, there is another branch that scientists called ornithiscia, the bird-hipped dinosaurs. Apparently, millions of years passed before the bird-hipped dinosaurs joined their lizard-hipped cousins.

Lesothosaurus, a little creature no bigger than a small dog, was like a test model for the big bird-hipped plant-eaters. It had short front feet, a thin body, and strong back legs that may have helped it to be a fast runner. Pisanosaurus, one of the first true bird-hipped dinosaurs, had a tail as long as its body. It stood on two feet and weighed about as much as a chicken.

The first bird-hipped dinosaurs walked on their back legs, but as they began to eat more and their bellies grew larger, they were forced to use all four feet to support this extra weight. If you believe that birds evolved from dinosaurs,

Try This

Dinosaur Sculptures

How about making a dinosaur out of boxes? All you need is a large box, two medium-sized boxes, several small boxes, and two rolls of masking tape. First place the large box on the ground to be the body, then tape the medium boxes in place to be the head and neck. Tape the smaller boxes on for the tail and legs.

Try This

Candy Cupcake Dinosaurs

To make a candy cupcake dinosaur, take an unfrosted cupcake and place it face down on a plate. Then frost the cupcake and add a large marshmallow for the dinosaur's head. To make the dinosaur's bumps, you can use gumdrops; for its scales, you can use wafer candies. You can use licorice for its tail and sprinkles for texture.

33

Words to Know

Triassic:

The word *Triassic* comes from the word *tri*, which means "three." There were three types of rock that were common during this time of the dinosaurs: sandstone, mudstone, and shale. Scientists now refer to this particular time period as Triassic.

you might think that they came from this side of the family. However, strange as it may seem, most scientists believe that birds descended from the saurischian (lizard-hipped) dinosaurs!

It's Not a Bird

Many of the old insects disappeared before the age of the dinosaurs, but grasshoppers and beetles took their place. Insects have continued to thrive and have survived through all the massive extinctions since that time. One of the reasons that the insects were so successful was that they could fly. No animal was able to do this until the pterosaurs, the huge bird-like reptiles, took to the air in the mid–**Triassic** Period.

One of the pterosaurs, Anurognathus, had a wingspan of around 20 inches, but only weighed about as much as a hummingbird. It ate insects, but probably not those huge dragonflies you read about earlier! Some of the later pterosaurs had big sail-like crests on their heads. If you want to see how this might have felt, ask someone who has a collection of baseball caps if you can try an experiment with them. Stack the hats on your head, adding one on top of another. Try walking around, then add a few more hats and try again, until you feel like you might tip over or until they start falling off. If your friends want to try this, have a competition!

Who am I?

I earned my name by being enormous. When I sat down to dinner I preferred to eat meat, lots of meat. I made my home in the world during the Jurassic time.
Who am I?

Megalosaurus

What's for Lunch?

After the giant island of Pangaea came together, the world was much warmer than it had been. These warmer temperatures would have made the per-

34

fect place for cold-blooded creatures to live. A crocodile-like reptile, the Phytosaur, was the top killer of the period. If you could have asked it what it wanted for lunch, the answer would have been "almost anything." Some dinosaurs were picky eaters, while other dinosaurs ate everything that moved. **Many of the dinosaurs could get by eating a little at a time, while others had to eat all day long just to survive.**

Can You Find It?

Many of the animals that lived during the age of the dinosaurs were labeled as killers, but other people believe that they were more like scavengers, feeding on the weakest animals and eating dead dinosaurs. If you want to go on a scavenger hunt like the dinosaurs, how about looking for some of the animals that you have learned about? For the next few weeks, keep

Words to Know

Pangaea:

Pangaea is the name given to the lands of the earth at the time when they came together to form one continent millions of years ago. The name Pangaea means "all earth." Scientists have found clues from fossils that show that the dinosaurs existed at this time.

Prehistoric Protection

The following riddle is missing five important letters. See if you can fit the letters from the bottom of the page into the correct blanks. HINT: The green dots are the spaces between words.

Is·i_·_ru_·_ha_·a
·_el_cirap__r·
w_n'_·a__ack·if·
__u·ar_·carr_ing
·a·_r__·branch?

_ha_·d_p_nds·_n
·h_w·fas_·__u·
carr_·i_!

E   T   V   Y   O

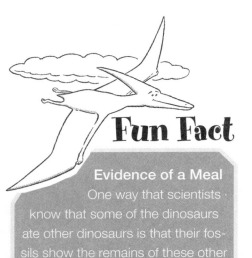

Fun Fact

Evidence of a Meal

One way that scientists know that some of the dinosaurs ate other dinosaurs is that their fossils show the remains of these other dinosaurs still in the stomach of the dinosaur that ate it.

Words to Know

carnivorous

When an animal is carnivorous, it means that he likes to eat meat or the flesh of other animals. Several of the dinosaurs were carnivores, including Tyrannosaurus rex.

your eyes open and see if you can find frogs, toads, snakes, or salamanders. Don't capture them! Instead, take a picture or write down where you saw them. Ask your friends if they want to join in the challenge. Also see who can find the most pictures of reptiles, amphibians, or dinosaurs in a magazine.

Is It a Bird, Reptile, or Mammal?

There were mammal-like reptiles before the Triassic Period and the age of the dinosaurs. Some of these creatures looked like reptiles; you might have thought that the one called the Dimetrodon looked like a dragon! It had an enormous sail on its back made from skin stretched over bones. It also had long fangs and it ate large animals.

Over time, other animals called cynodonts became more like mammals. Some of them were like our cows and pigs and they ate plants. Others looked like wolves and they were **carnivorous**, so they ate all types of meat, including reptiles and other cynodonts. Some scientists believe that they were warm-blooded.

The cynodonts had fur coats that they no longer needed when the temperature kept rising. In fact, they apparently started to tunnel under the ground to keep cool. They also started to decrease in size, so that they could hide from these new hunters, the dinosaurs. As the age of the dinosaurs went on, the mammal-like reptiles, some of which had been more than 5 feet long, became as small as a rat. Though the dinosaurs eventually became bigger, the mammal-like reptiles did not start increasing in size again until the dinosaurs were gone. After the dinosaurs became extinct, these animals evolved into what we call actual mammals, or the furry animals similar to those we see today. Some of them that live in the ocean, such as the whales, can weigh as much as ten full-grown elephants. Other mammals that remained on the

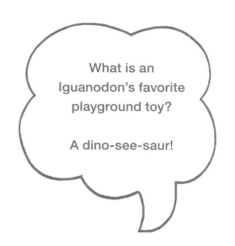

What is an Iguanodon's favorite playground toy?

A dino-see-saur!

Raptor Rebus

Figure out what word each picture puzzle represents, and you will learn the answers to these riddles! HINT: The black squares are the spaces between words.

When can three Velociraptors get under an umbrella and not get wet?

W + 🐔 ■ 🧤 – M – 10 + S

■ 🪢 ■ 🌧️

Where was the Velociraptor when the sun went down?

📍 – P ■ the 🏠

■ D +

Which One?

By my name you might think I was more of a dog than a bird. I became extinct during the same time that many other birds vanished from the earth as well. Which one am I?

A. Columbian Grebe
B. Bubal Hartebeest
C. Cape Lion
D. Labrador Duck

D. Labrador Duck

Fun Fact

Dry Land

Much of the earth was a desert during the Triassic Period. Today, the earth still contains several deserts; they make up around one-fifth of the earth's surface.

land still burrow in the earth today. Some examples are the foxes, coyotes, and weasels.

Tunneling

You can make your own tunnels out of large boxes. You may need an adult's help to open both ends of each box like doors. To make the tunnel, tape the boxes together in a line with all of the doors matching up so you can go all the way through from one end to the other. If you want to have a tunnel race, have someone use a watch to time each person in your group, as each of you crawls through the tunnel as fast as you can. Who has the quickest time? Does practice help? Try timing yourself for several days in a row. Can you beat your old time?

A Changing World

Through extinction and evolution, some animals disappear and others grow stronger. Dinosaurs appeared in the mid–Triassic Period, but they were not a dominant species until after a second extinction occurred between the Triassic and Jurassic periods.

The environment was changing, but for some reason, this helped the dinosaurs and they dominated the earth until the last mass extinction, which occurred 65 million years ago. Amphibians were evolving, too. Frogs, newts, and salamanders didn't appear on the earth until millions of years after the beginning of the age of the dinosaurs.

Chapter 4

Jurassic Jungle

Words to Know

Jurassic:
Many of the rocks discovered in the area of the Jura Mountains, located between Switzerland and France, were from a certain era long ago in the past. Scientists chose the name *Jurassic* to indicate the period of time the rocks came from.

Fun Fact

Jungles of Today
There are still places in the world today that are similar to the jungles of the dinosaurs. The rain forests are filled with different plants, animals, birds, and insects. Many rare reptiles and amphibians can be found living in these giant jungles.

Ferocious Fighters

When the carnosaurs, or "flesh lizards," appeared on the scene in the **Jurassic** times, there was no question about who was the king of that jungle.

One of these carnosaurs, Allosaurus, was the size of a large bus, weighed as much as a rhinoceros, and had teeth about 4 inches long! How would you like to live in the same world with this dinosaur? Scientists also think the Allosaurus hunted in groups or packs. There would be no doubt who would win when it came to the larger and more ferocious dinosaurs like this one.

Two other dinosaurs, known as Ceratosaurus and Megalosaurus, were only half as big as Allosaurus, but they probably could have ambushed larger dinosaurs and earned the title of winners if they wanted to. But usually, if they were unsuccessful at their hunting, they acted more like buzzards, which are the garbage collectors of our modern world, and ate whatever scraps or remains were left lying around. These reptiles were so strong, scientists came up with a new name for them—they called them **archosaurs.**

Dinosaur Wars

If you want to battle it out for the title of champion, you can have your own dinosaur wars by using squirt guns and paper cups with dinosaur pictures taped or drawn

on them. Set up the cups on a picnic table about 6 feet away from the line where you will stand with your squirt gun. The person who knocks the most cups off the table in two minutes wins.

You can also challenge all of your family and friends to this shootout to see who will be the top shooter, by seeing who can knock off five dinosaurs in the least amount of time.

Gentle Giants

Have you ever noticed how some people don't look much like their brothers and sisters, even though they are from the same family? Fossil hunters, who many times have only pieces of bone to look at, may think they have found a member of another dinosaur family when they have only found another sibling of a dinosaur that has already been found. After the dinosaur known as Apatosaurus had been discovered, the same hunter named another fossil Brontosaurus only to discover that they were both the same type of animal. Once this was figured out, the original name of Apatosaurus was given back to it.

Making Your Own Giant Dinosaur

If you want to make your own giant dinosaur to decorate your room, all you will need is an overhead projector, a plastic transparency sheet (or use a clear photo album page), a large piece of paper, a marker, and a picture of a dinosaur from a book or magazine. First you will want to trace the dinosaur picture onto your plastic with the marker. Then you can lay the plastic sheet on the overhead projector, and shine it onto a large piece of paper on the wall. Then trace your enlarged dinosaur onto the paper. When you're through,

Who am I?

You may know me by the horn on my head. I liked to walk around on my two back legs during the Jurassic time. My name sounds like a girl's name even though I could be a boy dinosaur, too!

Who am I?

Ceratosaurus

Words to Know

archosaur:
Archosaur means "ruling reptile." Dinosaurs were members of this group of reptiles, which also included pterosaurs and crocodiles. Crocodiles are the only members of the archosaur family that are still living today.

Which One?

I had a name that only had three letters in it. Two of the letters were vowels. While I was here on the earth, I was one of the largest flightless birds around. Which one am I?

A. Great Auk
B. Moa
C. Mysterious Starling
D. Night Heron

B. Moa

Try This

It's a Long Way Up

Scientists believe that some of the dinosaurs may have had trunks like those of the elephants and mammoths. If you want to see what it would be like to have a trunk, put a drinking straw in your mouth and try to pick up something light by breathing in through the straw. Try a piece of paper, a styrofoam cup, or a Ping-Pong ball. What else can you pick up?

you can take it off the wall to color or paint the dinosaur and then hang it up in your room.

Camouflaged Cover

One of the ways a dinosaur could fight for its life would be to run for cover. From some of the fossils that have been found, we can see that like many of today's lizards and snakes, certain dinosaurs may have been camouflaged, making them almost invisible in certain hiding places. If you were going out to play hide and seek and you wanted to camouflage yourself so you could hide better by blending in with the background, you could have an adult help you use different colored face paints and clothing to match the setting. Use black for night, brown for mud, green for the grass or trees, and tan for the sand and beach.

Just Imagine

For many years, scientists believed that the Brachiosaurus was so large that it needed a second brain. They thought this brain was located above its hips and that it might have helped the dinosaur to move its legs. Then they decided that what they had found was not another brain, but just a large bump on its spinal cord. The Brachiosaurus also had holes for nostrils in its forehead above its eyes. For many years, some scientists believed that these dinosaurs went under the water to eat and breathed through the nostril holes, which would have been just above the surface of the water. Scientists no longer believe that dinosaurs could survive with their bodies under that much water pressure, so now they are wondering if maybe there was a trunk fastened to these holes! Elephants have holes in almost the same spot on their heads.

The Brachiosaurus already was very tall, but that extra reaching tool might have made it possible to reach the very best leaves in the top of the tree. Would the dinosaur have used a trunk as a fifth limb? Do you think he might have used it to cool himself off on those hot days at the beach?

How do you think you would look if your arms were longer than your legs? Like a gorilla? The long-necked Brachiosaurus, who also had really long front legs and weighed about as much as fifteen elephants, was one of the dinosaurs that apparently could sit on his back legs, like a puppy. This way it could eat from the tops of trees whenever it wanted to. This dinosaur and many of the other

Full Plates

Break the letter-shifting code by writing the letters either one before or one after the letters shown on each of the Stegosaurus's plates.

When you have written in the correct letters, you will have the answer to the riddle.

What do you call a dinosaur who makes noise as he sleeps?

Heads or Tails

Place each of the words into the boxes in alphabetical order, starting across the top row and working your way down to the bottom row. When you're finished, read down the shaded column to answer to this riddle:

What does a Triceratops sit on? Its . . .

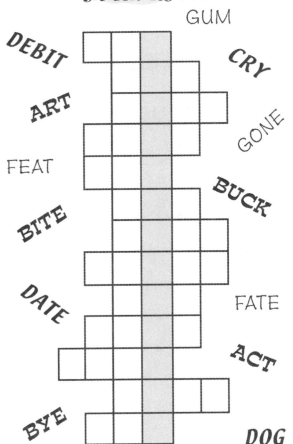

GUM

DEBIT

CRY

ART

GONE

FEAT

BUCK

BITE

DATE

FATE

ACT

BYE

DOG

sauropods (which means "lizard feet") liked to eat the soft leaves from the tops of the trees rather than the older leaves that were closer to the bottom. Some dinosaur experts wonder if this is why the sauropods and their necks kept growing bigger and longer as they evolved. Because of their size and their long necks, they were able to reach food that others couldn't.

Jungle Food Relay

Several fruits grow in the jungles, including bananas, starfruit, mangoes, and coconuts. If you have any of these fruits, you can have a dinosaur jungle food relay. Many of the dinosaurs had only two fingers on their hands, so for this race you will need to pick up and carry your fruit using just two fingers from each of your hands. (Thumbs don't count on this one—fingers only!) To begin the relay, divide the players into two groups. Then divide each group in half. Now have each group line up so one half of each group faces the other half. The two sides should stand 20 paces apart from each other.

When you are ready to start, place one fruit in front of each team. When you say "go," the first person on each team picks up the fruit with two fingers from each hand and carries it over to the other half of the team. Everyone takes a turn running the fruit to the other side. Once each person carries the fruit across, he or she should sit down. The first team that has all of their members sitting wins. For some variety you could carry the fruits other ways, such as balancing them on your head, or rolling them with your nose.

Tasty Eggsample

Sauropods, the mighty longnecks, had the largest eggs of any of the dinosaurs. One egg was probably close to a foot long and at least fifty times as big as a chicken egg. This recipe for creamed eggs on toast will make a great lunch for two people. How many people do you think you could feed if you could use one of those sauropod eggs?

To try this egg recipe, you will need three chicken eggs, a little butter, salt, milk, and four slices of bread. You also will need to ask an adult to help you boil the eggs and cook the milk sauce.

1. Boil the eggs for 10 minutes. Set them aside to cool, and then peel them and cut them into small pieces.
2. Melt ¼ cup butter in a medium-sized pan on low heat on top of the stove.
3. Add 1 rounded tablespoon of flour and ⅛ teaspoon salt to the butter, and stir until mixed well.
4. Add 2 cups of milk slowly and cook over medium heat until thickened.
5. Cut up whites of eggs, add to the milk mixture, and let simmer on low heat.
6. Toast four slices of bread and top them with the egg mixture.
7. Crumble egg yolks over toast and eggs mixture. Serve hot.

Who am I?

I am a dinosaur who has been studied greatly. You might know me by the two rows or walls of bone that run down the middle of my head. I had very sharp claws on my fingers and toes. I also had a whip-like tail.

Who am I?

Allosaurus

Which One?

Because of my size, I would never have fit into a cage, or even a tree for that matter. I actually could have made an ostrich look small if I stood next to one. You might think I would like peanuts if I were still around. Which one am I?

A. Guam Flycatcher
B. Xerces Blue Butterfly
C. Elephant Bird
D. Short-tailed Hopping Mouse

C. Elephant Bird

Who am I?

I was one of the first dinosaurs to be found. I was named for my lizard-like teeth. The lizard I was named for is still around today. Many people think that I used to walk around on three of my toes.

Who am I?

Iguanodon

Fun Fact

How Small?

As new dinosaurs are discovered each year, the record for the smallest dinosaur keeps changing. The dinosaur now thought to be the smallest is Micropachycephalosaurus, whose skeleton measures less than 2 feet long.

Giant Food Problems

Did the sauropod dinosaurs become extinct because they had weak or bad teeth that were only good for scraping off leaves? Many sauropod fossil skeletons have been found with stones known as gastroliths in their stomach area. They were only able to digest their food by swallowing these "stomach stones," which helped grind up the food in their stomachs. Today, chickens have a digestive organ called a gizzard that's filled with tiny stones to grind up their food.

Scientists think that the plant-eaters spent most of each day collecting their food, and some of them needed up to 300 pounds of food each day to survive. This need for so much food leaves the scientists wondering how any animal with such a small head on such a huge body could ever gather enough to eat!

Miniature Monsters

If you could see a picture of Compsognathus, the dinosaur known as "pretty jaw," you might wonder if the fossil hunter who named it had a very vivid imagination. Its head was more delicate than most of the other meat-eaters and you couldn't see its sharp teeth, but it definitely was a killer. It also had a delicate body, weighing as little as a large chicken, but it was as tall as a young human teenager. The geckoes or chameleons that you can find in a pet store look a lot like a very small version of this dinosaur.

Some fossil hunters in Germany once thought that they had found another Compsognathus fossil, until they discovered that it had wings, feathers, and feet that could perch on a tree branch! It turned out they had discovered a new dinosaur called Archaeopteryx. Even though the Archaeopteryx

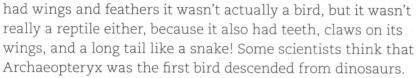
had wings and feathers it wasn't actually a bird, but it wasn't really a reptile either, because it also had teeth, claws on its wings, and a long tail like a snake! Some scientists think that Archaeopteryx was the first bird descended from dinosaurs.

There were not very many small meat-eating dinosaurs in the Jurassic Period. Ornitholestes, who was one of them, only weighed as much as a medium-sized dog, but its long, curved claws and sharp teeth made it easy for it to eat its food. It was nicknamed the "bird robber," because some fossil hunters believed its diet consisted of early birds like Archaeopteryx. However, none of the Ornitholestes and Archaeopteryx fossils have been found in the same place, so now this is no longer believed to be true.

Who makes the best Jurassic-style clothes?

A dino-sewer!

Sharp Enough

Although the dinosaurs weren't necessarily considered sharp, their claws were. Several of the dinosaurs had claws, including the Velociraptor, Utahraptor, and the Troodon. Can you think of any other animal that has claws? Dogs do, and so do cats. Even humans have nails that they can use for several things, including scratching an itch.

How many things can you think of that are sharp? How about playing a game of "Hang Dinosaur" using sharp things for the clues? You can draw a hangman stand on a chalkboard and then add the blanks that represent each letter of a word, such as _ _ _ _ _ for claws. The other players can guess letters they think are in your word. For each guess that is wrong you can draw a part of the dinosaur on the stand.

Fun Fact

No Bones About It!

Although numerous dinosaur bones have been found in the ground all over the world, very few bones have been found under the sea. The ocean may be hiding several types of dinosaur we have never seen before.

Try This

Who Has Horns?

Several of the dinosaurs had horns. Can you think of their names? Now how about making a list of all of the animals with horns living in the world today? Try this quiz on your friends. Whose list is the longest?

If the players guess the answer first, they win. If you draw the complete dinosaur first, you win.

Come Closer

Some of the smaller dinosaurs were only about the size of some of the reptiles we see today. These dinosaurs were so small compared to the larger dinosaurs that the larger dinosaurs, such as Tyrannosaurus rex, may not have even noticed them.

Have you ever looked through a magnifying glass? This is a tool that makes it possible for us to see items so small we might not notice them otherwise. To take a closer look at your world, you can go on a microscopic walk. If you don't have a magnifying glass of your own, see if you can borrow one from someone you know. Then take a walk around your neighborhood to get a closer look at the creatures who live in the grass, dirt, or flowers. You may find there are a lot more things out there than you first thought.

Plated Puzzles

The plated dinosaurs were some of the last and most unusual varieties of dinosaurs to appear in the Jurassic period. The bodies of Scelidosaurus and Scutellosaurus were covered with small plates like a sort of flexible armor. Scientists think that these dinosaurs could have been the ancestors of either the Stegosaurus or the Anklyosaurus.

You might be mad if someone called you a birdbrain, but you should be more upset if they called you a Stegosaurus-brain. Why? Because a Stegosaurus's body was larger than the biggest van, yet its brain was probably only the size of a walnut. Scientists used to think that the Stegosaurus, like

the Brachiosaurus, had a second brain located in the area above its hips that helped control its legs, but they found out that wasn't true. Almost everything about the Stegosaurus was different from other dinosaurs, including its tail, which was longer than the rest of its body and covered with long spikes at the end. Its name, "roofed lizard," comes from the huge plates that scientists first believed covered its back like tiles on a roof. Because its bones were in a pile when paleontologists found them, scientists aren't sure how the plates were arranged. They also wonder if the plates were colored like a rainbow to attract or frighten other dinosaurs, or if they were used like solar panels to warm up the Stegosaurus on cold mornings.

Try This

Chalk Dinosaurs

You can use chalk to draw dinosaurs on your sidewalk. All you need are a few pictures for inspiration and a box of colored chalk. If you want to draw with chalk inside your house, try dipping your chalk in a small dish of milk (with an adult's permission!) and painting on glossy paper.

Puzzle Master

How good are you at putting these pieces together to see what kind of dinosaur you have discovered? Copy square 1A into empty box 1A in the grid. Then copy square 2A and so on until you have a complete dinosaur. What have you found?

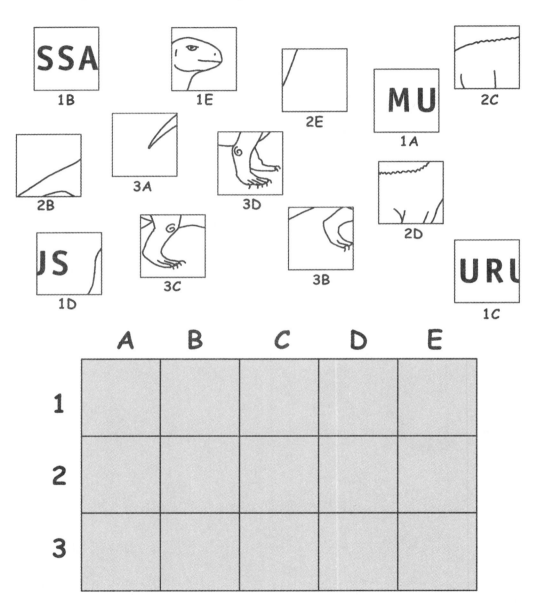

Stegosaurus's cousin, the Kentrosaurus, whose fossils were found in Germany, had many more spikes than did Stegosaurus. The Kentrosaurus's spikes seem to have run all the way from the tip of its tail to the top of its hips, rather than being only at the end of the tail like the Stegosaurus.

Putting It All Together

If you want to see what it might be like to be a dinosaur hunter, you can try to piece together a dinosaur of your own. All you need is a large picture of a dinosaur, maybe from an old magazine or poster that you can cut apart. Always ask an adult first if it's okay for you to cut out a picture. Then carefully cut the picture into pieces of different shapes, so it will turn out sort of like a puzzle. Now, once you have the picture in pieces, try putting it back together again. Can your family figure it out and solve your puzzle? How about your friends—how quickly can they figure out which part goes where? To make things trickier, find a bunch of pictures, cut them apart with your friends, and then trade so that everyone is putting together someone else's dinosaur puzzle. Can you figure out how it goes together even if you don't know exactly what it looked like in the first place? That's what real dinosaur hunters try to do all the time.

Together Again

When the real dinosaurs got together, they may have acted like elephants, working together to find food and shelter, or they may have acted more like cats, finding almost

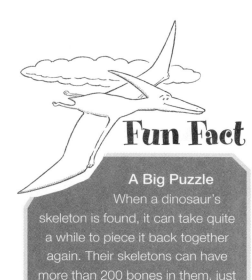

Fun Fact

A Big Puzzle

When a dinosaur's skeleton is found, it can take quite a while to piece it back together again. Their skeletons can have more than 200 bones in them, just like ours. Putting something back together when you have never seen it before could be sort of puzzling.

What do you get if you cross a pig with a dinosaur?

Jurassic Pork!

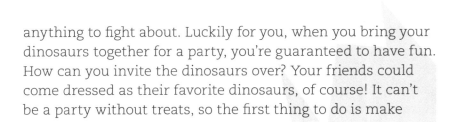
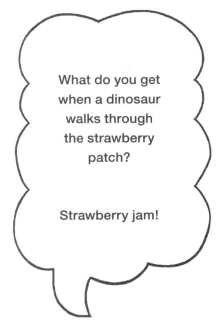

What do you get when a dinosaur walks through the strawberry patch?

Strawberry jam!

What type of tool does a Jurassic carpenter use?

A dino-saw

anything to fight about. Luckily for you, when you bring your dinosaurs together for a party, you're guaranteed to have fun. How can you invite the dinosaurs over? Your friends could come dressed as their favorite dinosaurs, of course! It can't be a party without treats, so the first thing to do is make something to eat.

Dinosaurs liked the mud, so you could make a mud pie. With an adult's help, fill a graham cracker crust with chocolate pudding. You might also want to have a can of whipped cream so your dinosaur friends can add topping to the mud pie. For games, you could start by trying to guess what kind of dinosaur each person is. Then you could hold four-legged, three-legged, and two-legged relays. For a four-legged relay, you need three people for each team. The person in the middle has his left leg tied to the right leg of the person on his left side, and his right leg tied to the left leg of the person on his right. In a three-legged relay, one person's left leg is tied to another person's right leg, and in a two-legged relay everyone runs on their own. Be sure to have an adult to help you with the tying and to supervise the race!

How about a dino hunt? You can hide several plastic dinosaurs and give your friends a map of where to try to find them. You also can challenge them to a game of dinosaur toss, to see who can get a stuffed dinosaur through a hoop that you ask an adult to hang from a tree.

Chapter 5
Cretaceous Creatures

Words to Know

cretaceous:
The word *cretaceous* means having chalk or chalk-like qualities. During the cretaceous time of the dinosaurs, the land was filled with rocks made of chalk or limestone.

Who am I?

The beginning of my name means "three." You might recognize me by the horns I had on my head; two above my eyes and one on the end of my nose. I was one of the Cretaceous dinosaurs that walked on four feet.

Who am I?

Triceratops

Lots of Growing and Changing

The **Cretaceous** Period was a time of change. Pangaea was becoming a group of islands again and the temperature was dropping. A number of flowering plants appeared, including today's magnolia tree, and bees started to pollinate those flowers. As Pangaea slowly split apart, the dinosaurs became stranded on the drifting continents.

Many of the dinosaurs did disappear during this time and others could only be found in certain places, but overall the numbers, sizes, and varieties of dinosaurs were greater than they had ever been before.

There had been very few large predatory dinosaurs in the Triassic and Jurassic periods, but during the Cretaceous Period, there began to be many more as a result of a huge increase in the number of large plant-eaters. Bird-hipped dinosaurs came in all shapes and sizes in the Cretaceous period. A group known as the iguanodontids were thought to have appeared at the end of the Jurassic Period, but grew larger during the Cretaceous Period, and soon could be found on most of the continents. Some of them weighed as much as three elephants, and they had much more efficient teeth than the earlier long necks. The duckbilled dinosaurs also descended from this group.

How Do You Eat Your Leaves?

Today, giraffes grab leaves with their long tongues and then pull the leaves off of the trees. The fossils of some of these leaf-eating dinosaurs have what looks like a big dent in their lower jaws, which makes scientists wonder if they also possessed long tongues and used them in the same way.

The Cretaceous ornithopods, which means "bird foot" in Greek, had teeth that could grind up their plant food before it ever reached their stomach. Earlier plant-eaters had to swallow the leaves whole after they bit them off the trees.

The Most Efficient Plant-Eaters

At the end of the Cretaceous Period, a new type of plant-eater appeared, called the duckbills or hadrosaurs. The duckbills had a beak like a duck and a tail like a crocodile. Because of this, scientists used to think that the duckbills spent most of their time in the water. Now they believe they just lived close to it. They had even better teeth than the dinosaurs that came before them, but their teeth were not located in the front of their duckbilled mouth. The duckbills had teeth that were located at the sides of the mouth—hundreds of upper and lower teeth that rubbed against each other. The duckbills would use these teeth to grind their food before they swallowed it. These special teeth would fall out and grow back constantly. There were as many as 1,000 teeth in a duckbill's mouth at one time!

Edible Dinosaur

If you want to make a dinosaur's head that you can eat, all you need is a Twinkie or other small cake of the same shape, some green frosting, and a few decorations. With a plastic knife, slice the cake partly in half lengthwise, separating the top from the bottom about three-fourths of the way back. Then spread the frosting over the outside. Next, pry the cake apart in the front and stick in small marshmallows for the dinosaur's teeth. On top of the back of the cake add two large marshmallow halves using frosting to stick the

Who am I?

You may know me best by what looks like a cap on my head. Or you may think you would need to hide your eggs from me.
Who am I?

Oviraptor

Try This

Remember to Chew Your Food!

Some dinosaurs had several different types of teeth, just as we do. Some of their teeth were for tearing, some were for cutting, and others were for grinding. Have you ever tried to bite something in half using your side teeth? How about trying to chew your food using just your front teeth? Can you chew on just one side?

 55

Who am I?

By my name, you might think
that I liked to live in a tent
or roast marshmallows.
I lived in both the Jurassic
and Cretaceous periods.
I liked to walk around with
my tail sticking straight
out behind me.
Who am I?

Camptosaurus

How do you know
if there's a dinosaur
under your bed?

Your nose hits
the ceiling!

marshmallows on the cake and the candy pieces on to be the dinosaur's pupils.

The Noise Makers

The second type of the duckbilled hadrosaurs had crests. Some of the crests looked like small little hatchets, helmets, or horns attached to the dinosaurs' heads. At first some scientists believed that the duckbilled dinosaurs lived in the water, so it only seemed reasonable to think that these dinosaurs used the tubes or openings in their heads like snorkels to take in air when they put their heads underwater. After studying them a little closer they realized that the tubes were not open at both ends. So what were they for?

Maybe these tubes, like those of the Parasaurolophus, were connected to its throat and lungs. Some dinosaur lovers think that the tubes may have been used to make a variety of sounds. What sounds do you think these dinosaurs would make? Quacks, honks, or maybe some type of horn-like sound?

What Big Teeth You Have!

The lizard-hipped meat-eaters came in all shapes and sizes, too. If asked to name the fiercest dinosaur, most people would probably say it was Tyrannosaurus rex (T. rex). With a skull that was more than 4 feet long, and about fifty teeth sticking out of its mouth, it must have been a scary sight to see! The teeth were close to 8 inches long and the mouth was large enough to swallow an adult human body standing straight up.

Fossil hunters have found a smaller dinosaur that they named Nanotyrannus, which means "pygmy tyrant." It would take nine more of these dinosaurs standing on top of this one to reach the size of T. rex. Do you think this is really a new type of dinosaur, or could it be an earlier T. rex or maybe a baby?

The Tyrannosaurus rex isn't the only dinosaur you would have tried to stay away from. Carcharodontosaur, named after the great white shark, and Gigantosaurus, named for its size, were longer than a T. rex, weighed more, and had teeth that were just as large. There were other large dinosaurs that looked more like huge ostriches. Just like the bears, wolves, and coyotes of today, these dinosaurs staked out their own territory and kept the animal populations from increasing too much by hunting in the area around them.

It's a Dinosaur-Eat-Dinosaur World!

Would you believe that for many years, the main items on a meat-eating dinosaur's menu were insects, small reptiles, mammals, eggs, and probably even baby dinosaurs? When the huge meat-eaters appeared in the Jurassic Period, those animals were definitely eating other dinosaurs!

Many dinosaurs ate only meat, or only plants. But did you know there are other dinosaurs that eat both? These dinosaurs are called **omnivorous** because they liked to eat more than one type of food.

Fun Fact

Size Isn't Everything

Did you know that size isn't always the most important thing? You might think that when it came to fighting, the biggest dinosaur always won. This wasn't always true. Some of the largest dinosaurs lost their battles to a smaller, more aggressive dinosaur or a group of them.

Which One?

I used to be one of the most common birds around. My first name might have you thinking that I liked to ride long when you went places. There are still other birds with my last name. Which one am I?

A. Night Heron
B. Passenger Pigeon
C. Mysterious Starling
D. Dusky Seaside Sparrow

B. Passenger Pigeon

Dino-mite!

Unscramble the words at the bottom of the page. Then write the words in the proper places to complete each of the following dino riddles.

Careful—there is one more answer word than you will need!

What do you call it when a sauropod slides into home base?

Dino_____

What do you call a Plesiosaur that talks and talks and talks?

Dino_____

What was the Tyrannosaurus rex after lifting weights?

Dino_____

Where do Pterosaurs like to go on vacation?

Dino_____

Where did the Velociraptor do her holiday shopping?

Dino_____

Which dinosaurs are the best policemen?

Tricera_____

What do you get if you cross a Triceratops with a kangaroo?

Tricera_____

broe   pcos   rsteo

        rsoe   opdrs

ohers   phos   orsce

Hunting Prey

Have you seen hawks, owls, and eagles circling in the air, waiting to snatch up small animals below? They belong to a group of birds known as raptors. Millions of years ago, there were a number of earthbound dinosaurs that hunted in a similar way. They also are known as raptors.

For many years, scientists believed that dinosaurs had very little intelligence and were cold-blooded reptiles. However, the size of the skull in the fossils of dinosaur raptors like Deinonychus and Troodon indicate that they were probably capable of planning and carrying out group attacks on the much larger plant-eaters. From looking at the fossils, scientists think that the dinosaur raptors had large eyes, which

Words to Know

omnivorous:

When an animal is omnivorous, it likes to eat both plants and meat. Most humans are omnivorous, and so were many of the dinosaurs. The Oviraptor was an omnivorous dinosaur.

Words to Know

prey:
When one animal hunts another animal, the animal that is being hunted is called the prey. Many of the smaller dinosaurs were prey to the larger meat-eating dinosaurs.

usually means that an animal could see better in the dark. This led scientists to believe that the raptors were warm-blooded killers who spent the night searching for their cold-blooded victims, the reptiles. Deinonychus had an out-sized claw on each back foot that never touched the ground unless he needed to extend it to wound his **prey**.

One of the strangest discoveries ever made by dinosaur hunters was a part of a dinosaur that only included the arms of a new type of raptor, or dinosaur with claws. The arms were about 8½ feet long, which would be longer than the average couch. This means you probably wouldn't have wanted to meet the monster that would have been attached to those arms!

What is noisier than a Hadrosaurus?

Color in the shapes that contain the letters N-O-I-S-E and you will find out!

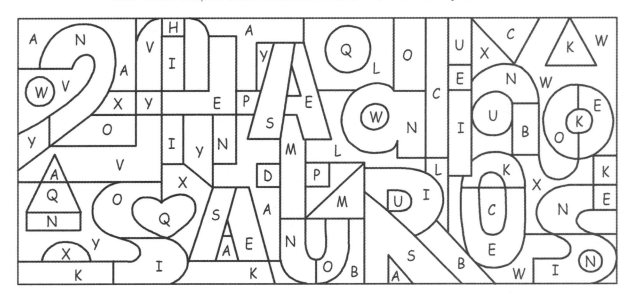

Look Out Above!

During this time the tiny pterosaurs had evolved into huge, gliding fish hunters that were now half as big as a small plane. They could ride on currents of warm air rising up from the earth, which are called thermals. The pterosaurs traveled for hundreds of miles and sometimes soared as high as 4 miles up into the air with only a flap or two of their wings. It is thought that they migrated for thousands of miles to return to the place where they were born. The slightest breeze could lift them high into the air and they would be flying, whether they wanted to or not.

Many scientists have compared these pterosaurs to the bat, a mammal that is alive today. Pterosaurs had claws on their wings to help them cling to trees and rocks, just as bats do. Also, like bats, the small pterosaurs were insect-eaters. We know that bats are constantly bothered by parasites, or bugs, and a lot of the research that has been done has left most scientists believing that dinosaurs, including the pterosaurs, also were plagued by parasites. Scientists have found one insect fossil that appears to have only one function, which was taking blood from other creatures. Can you think of any insects like that? The fossil that they found closely resembles a bat flea. Another fossil of a pterosaur shows markings that make us think that the pterosaurs were furry just like the bats, too, so it's very possible that the pterosaurs could have had fleas!

The pterosaurs also had another enemy. These were the true birds, which had evolved from the earlier bird-like dinosaurs when their scales gradually changed into feathers. Eventually these true birds attempted to take the pteorsaurs' home territories from them.

Which One?

When you hear my name you might think that I was more of a little devil than a wolf. I had a body like a dog and stripes like a tiger. Which one am I?

A. Giant Wallaby
B. Tasmanian Wolf
C. Dire Wolf
D. Arabian Gazelle

B. Tasmanian Wolf

Fun Fact

Hidden Eggs
Some crocodiles bury their eggs in the sand. Once the babies hatch and begin to make noise, they dig them back up again. Do you think the dinosaurs listened for their babies' cries?

 61

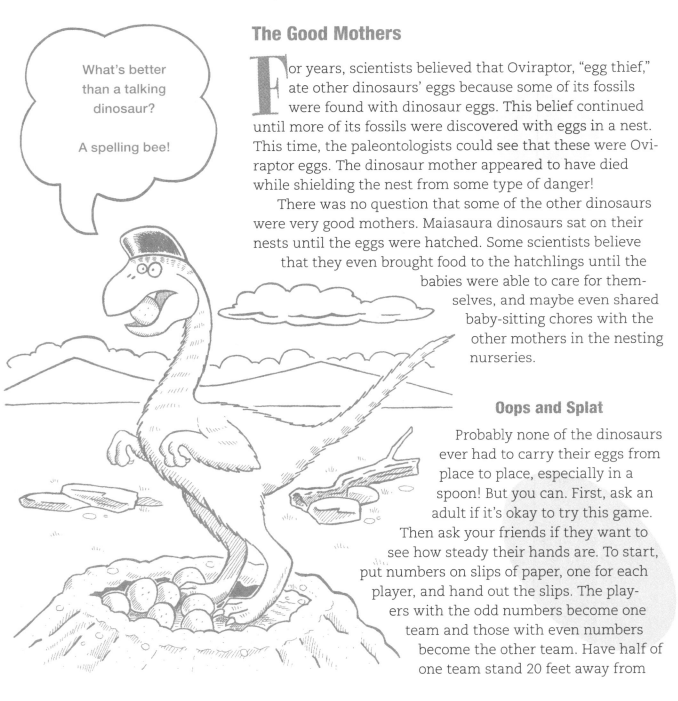

What's better than a talking dinosaur?

A spelling bee!

The Good Mothers

For years, scientists believed that Oviraptor, "egg thief," ate other dinosaurs' eggs because some of its fossils were found with dinosaur eggs. This belief continued until more of its fossils were discovered with eggs in a nest. This time, the paleontologists could see that these were Oviraptor eggs. The dinosaur mother appeared to have died while shielding the nest from some type of danger!

There was no question that some of the other dinosaurs were very good mothers. Maiasaura dinosaurs sat on their nests until the eggs were hatched. Some scientists believe that they even brought food to the hatchlings until the babies were able to care for themselves, and maybe even shared baby-sitting chores with the other mothers in the nesting nurseries.

Oops and Splat

Probably none of the dinosaurs ever had to carry their eggs from place to place, especially in a spoon! But you can. First, ask an adult if it's okay to try this game. Then ask your friends if they want to see how steady their hands are. To start, put numbers on slips of paper, one for each player, and hand out the slips. The players with the odd numbers become one team and those with even numbers become the other team. Have half of one team stand 20 feet away from

Curious Question

Collect all the Question (Q) words and write them in the Question space. Collect all the Answer (A) words and write them in the Answer space. Put the words in the correct order to get a curious question and its answer!

Q there	A to	Q old
A new	Q the	A they
Q dinosaur	A ones!	Q in
A afford	Q Why	Q only
Q are	A buy	Q museum?
A Because	Q bones	A can't

Question:

_____

Answer:

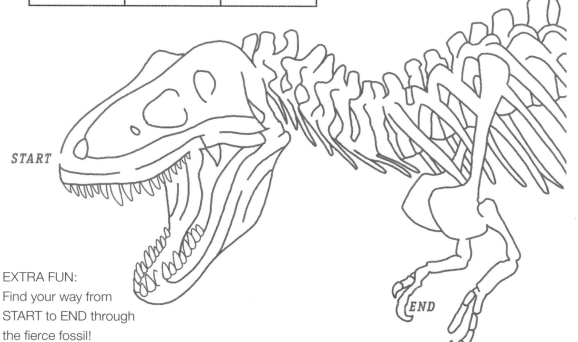

START

END

EXTRA FUN:
Find your way from
START to END through
the fierce fossil!

the other half, with the two sides facing each other. Have the other team move over 10 paces and do the same thing. Give the first person in each of the lines a spoon with a raw egg on it. Tell them to carry it to the other side of their team and hand the spoon to the next person. Each team should keep taking turns carrying the eggs back and forth until someone drops an egg or everyone has carried it to the other side. The fastest, safest egg carriers win!

Magical Eggs

If you wanted to make some special eggs for your egg race, you might try this experiment. You will need a clear glass container, a small plastic bag, a rubber band, vinegar, and an egg:

1. Put 1 cup of vinegar in your container.
2. Put an uncooked egg very carefully into the vinegar.
3. Cover your container with a small plastic bag and put the rubber band over the bag.
4. Check on your egg in an hour, in three hours, in a day, and in a week. Make sure you replace the bag and rubber band each time after checking your egg. What happened?

Armed with Armor

Just like the skeletons of today's wild animals, many of the fossilized bones show spines and horns. Pieces of skin clinging to some of the fossils show that many of the dinosaurs were armored or had bony plates that were mounted right into the skin itself.

Who am I?

You might expect to find me at the top of a beanstalk, living in a castle with a golden egg. That is, if I were in a dinosaur fairy tale.

Who am I?

Gigantosaurus

What do you get when a dinosaur sneezes?

Out of the way!

Cretaceous Creatures

When you think of a dinosaur, do you think of an enormous beast, something like a rhinoceros or a dragon? Proceratops, "first horned face," was the size of a pig, and when he hatched out of his egg, he looked like a toad with a tail. He had small lumps on his face and a bony bump on the back of his skull. As he grew up, a shield formed to cover the back of his neck. Wouldn't it be fun to see what a teenaged dinosaur looked like? Fossil hunters have found Proceratops of many ages, from babies to adults. Proceratops looked like a rhino because of its nose horn and like a parrot because of its beak. It also had a large neck frill that was probably used only to frighten its enemies.

Who am I?

I was one of the first dinosaurs that belonged to the horned dinosaur family. I had a fat tail that I held up high when I walked and a large beak that looked like a can opener.

Who am I?

Protoceratops

Have you ever heard of any other ceratopsians, or horned dinosaurs?

Triceratops had long horns growing above each eye. This dinosaur didn't have to worry if one of these three horns was lost in a fight. It quickly grew back again. There also was a dinosaur called a Pentaceratops. Because *penta* means "five," you would think that this dinosaur had five horns, but scientists believe that some of the bumps on its skull were just large cheekbones.

You probably wouldn't like it if someone called you thick-headed, but Pachycephalosaurus, a close cousin to the ceratopsians, certainly was. His skull could have been 10 inches thick, and he probably used it to butt heads just as today's goats or rams do. Ankylosaurus was a dinosaur that was built like a turtle and looked sort of like a small tank. What could be more frightening than a turtle with horns surrounding its body and a tail that could break a leg? His only weak spot was probably his stomach; even his eyelids were made of bone!

Following Their Lead

What animals can you think of that continue to protect themselves with armor today? The armadillo's name gives a hint. Then there are the alligators, crocodiles, turtles, tortoises, scorpions, lobsters, crabs, and all types of shellfish.

Can you think of something you see every day that gives this type of protection? What about bike and motorcycle helmets, or knee and elbow pads? Next time you put on your protective gear to ride your bike or play sports, you can imagine that you're a dinosaur in your very own suit of armor!

Chapter 6

Footprints from the Past

Why Do They Make Them This Way?

You probably haven't thought much about different types of shoes or the prints or **impressions** that they make. If you have thought about them, probably all you were interested in is how they look.

Have you ever looked at the soles of your shoes and wondered *why* they are made the way that they are? Were the designers trying to duplicate the bottom of an animal's foot so you could get better traction for climbing hills or to be able to run fast or stop quickly?

You could try playing a game of shoe-track hide-and-seek. To start, all you need are a few friends who are wearing pairs of old shoes. The object of the game is to follow the prints, so you will want to play in the sand or dirt where you can see tracks. (This also would be a great game to play in the winter, just after a fresh snowfall!) Everyone should take turns looking at the soles of each other's shoes or boots. Next, if you're the seeker, close your eyes and count to 100 while everyone else hides, and then start following the tracks. When you get close to the person who is hiding, stop and try to guess who it is by the shoe print. If you're right, that person becomes the next seeker.

Do you think the dinosaurs followed each other's tracks? Or do you think they found each other in different ways?

Feet Facts

When the dinosaurs were discovered, scientists divided them into classes by the type of hips and feet that they had. Plateosaurus was called a prosauropod, which means "before lizard feet"; it was considered by some scientists to be the link between the "beast-feet" theropods (like Megalosaurus) and the "lizard-feet" sauropods (like Apatosaurus).

Words to Know

impression:
An impression is a mark or print left behind on something by an object or animal that was there before. Fossil tracks, like those of the dinosaurs, are one type of impression.

Who am I?

They probably should have named me Unsure-a-saurus, because no one is really sure if the remains that they found were all mine or maybe parts of another dinosaur!
Who am I?

Ultrasaurus

All of these dinosaurs came before the "bird-feet" ornithopods (like Iguanodon). To make it even more confusing, prosauropods, theropods, and sauropods were all classed as "lizard-hipped" saurischians, and ornithopods were classed as "bird-hipped" ornithischians.

Whether they are labeled as beast, lizard, or bird feet, you would probably have to be a scientist to see much difference between these dinosaurs' tracks, other than the fact that the number of fingers and toes kept changing over the years and some of the claws changed into hooves.

Real Dinosaur Tracks?

In one place there are preserved dinosaur tracks that look as though the dinosaurs walked straight up a rock wall. This illusion was created when mountains rose, pushing a slab of stone that had once been part of a riverbed up into the air. One mystery that someone happened upon was a set of dinosaur tracks that appear to tell the story of a plant-eater being chased by a meat-eater. The real mystery is how the prints managed to remain there through all these years when they were made in soft mud. Normally, rain should have washed them away, unless there wasn't any more rain for a very long time.

If you would like to know more about visiting other places to see dinosaur fossils and prints, you can visit your library or go on your Internet search page and type in "dinosaur tracks" in your search box.

Fun Fact

State What?
Most states have a state flag, state flower, and state song, but did you know that several states have a state fossil? The state fossil of Colorado is the Stegosaurus.

Which One?

I was one of the biggest and slowest creatures around. Unlike all the other animals who have the same last name as I do, I never liked to be up in the trees. Which one am I?

A. Ground Sloth
B. Barbados Raccoon
C. Bali Tiger
D. Cuban Monkey

A. Ground Sloth

Tracking Them Down

Did you know that real-life detectives make plaster casts of footprints and tire tracks from a crime scene and then use them for evidence? They can use the casts to try to find out who has shoes or tires like the tracks that they found. To make a cast of a track, first ask an adult to help you gather a disposable cup, a disposable spoon, a plastic bag filled with dry plaster of Paris, a container of water, and a pair of disposable gloves. Once you find a track in the ground, pour your plaster of Paris in the cup, add enough water to make it like mud, stir it, and then pour it over the track and let it dry. When the plaster is dry, you can lift it up out of the ground and you will have a cast of the print.

Do You Believe in Giants?

When you look at your parents, they probably seem pretty tall to you, but can you imagine living in the same world with an animal that was so big that

just one vertebrae, which was one of the many pieces of its backbone, was as tall as an adult human? That dinosaur was called Seismosaurus, because he weighed so much that people think each step he took probably made the earth quake! Scientists can measure and record the vibrations that come from an earthquake by using seismographs. Do you think they would use them to warn us when the dinosaurs were coming near if the "great lizards" were still living today? Just imagine if you heard something that weighed twice as much as a semitrailer coming down a trail after you!

What happened when the dinosaur took the train home?

She had to bring it back!

How Do Scientists Know That Some Dinosaurs Were Professional Racers?

Cross out letters that appear more than five times in the letter grid. Read the remaining letters from left to right, and top to bottom.

```
T B G B H J G J E B J G M Y B G J F B J B O
J U M B J X N J M J D M B X X F M X M X O M
B M S X S G X B I B M M L J G M I G Z J G J
M G M J X J B M M B G X J M G M X J X B M E
D X G M D G X G J I M B M N X J B X O X J X
B M S X B X A M M X U M J M R X X M J T X G
J X G J M J M M B G X J J B X G J R M X B M
B G M J A X G X C X J K X G M J B X B M J S
```

71

Try This

Shake, Rattle, and Roll

One way you could check for dinosaurs or earthquakes in your neighborhood would be to make your own seismograph. All you need is a Styrofoam cup filled almost to the top with water. To see the motion in the water, try stomping on the ground near the cup or tapping on the surface of the table.

Who am I?

I am one of the most famous or well-known dinosaurs of all time. I was also one of the last dinosaurs to disappear from the earth.
Who am I?

Tyrannosaurus

Did You Feel That?

Have you ever been in a place where an earthquake was occurring? You might not even have known what was happening until someone told you, "That was an earthquake." Sometimes when an earthquake happens, you might only notice little things, like water moving in your glass. Other times, the earth quakes more noticeably. It all depends on the size of the earthquake. People who live in areas where earthquakes happen a lot are always preparing in case the next one will be a big one. When a large earthquake occurs, the land shifts and moves, changing many of the things in its path, such as buildings, roads, and bridges. That is why sometimes after an earthquake you will see broken sections of roads and torn-down buildings. These earthquakes are nothing new; they also happened during the dinosaurs' time on the earth. Think how scary it must have been to the dinosaurs to see chunks of rocks moving around without having any idea why this was happening!

An Appetite to Match Their Size

Have you ever been to the top of a six-story building? Sauroposeidon, named after Poseidon, the god of the sea, would have been able to look right into the top windows of that building! Some people think that Sauroposeidon ate leaves by swinging his neck around in a circle, because it would have been too much work to move his large body all of the time. This way, he could eat everything within his reach before moving on to the next bunch of trees. If you were that big, it would probably take a truckload of hamburgers and hot dogs to fill you up.

When the dinosaurs ate all of the tree leaves in their neighborhood, they had to keep moving to new sources of

Find the Fossil

Dr. Pole has just had a new discovery named after him! Use the following clues to discover which fossil is the "Poleumita."

- The Poleumita does not have wings.
- The fossil to the left of Poleumita is a tooth.
- The Poleumita is not broken in half.
- The Poleumita has a spiral pattern.

EXTRA FUN: Read the letters with the fossils from bottom to top, and right to left, and you will find the answer to this riddle:

What do you call a petrified T. Rex?

73

Try This

Dinosaurs Made of Sand

To make your sand dinosaurs, you can use sand or clay from a river or beach. You also can find sand at a local craft store. Put the sand in a dish or on a plate. Then use a plastic spoon, fork, or knife to make a sand picture. If you want your sand to stick together, you will need to add just enough water to make the sand damp.

What should you do if you find a dinosaur in your bed?

Find somewhere else to sleep!

enormous Goliath. Many of today's basketball players are certainly a lot bigger than the average adult is. A century ago, very few men were 6 feet tall, but now there are a lot of them.

In the past, when people grew more than 7 feet tall, it was usually due to something that was wrong with a gland in their necks called the pituitary gland. The pituitary gland has many purposes, but most people think of it as a "growth gland." Do you think that some of the dinosaurs had something wrong with their pituitary gland, or do you think they grew so big because of something that they ate?

If you could eat something that would make you a lot bigger, would you want to? Just for fun, you could get out your measuring tape and see how tall your friends and family are. Some people say that if you take the height you were when you were two years old and then you multiply that measurement times two, you will come up with the height you will be when you grow up. Maybe the dinosaurs doubled their size, too! If you want to test the theory of doubling our size from the age of two, ask your friends' families if they can remember or have records of how tall their children were. Or measure your brothers and sisters at that age, and wait to see if it comes true!

What About Dragons?

Have your parents read any fairy tales to you? Many fairy tales describe creatures that looked like flying dragons. For thousands of years, children all over the world have heard stories about dragons. Dinosaur hunters have found many dinosaur fossils in the same lands where the stories are told, and some of the dinosaurs certainly did look like dragons without wings. A pterosaur fossil looks a lot like a dragon because of its long tail, big teeth, and the claws on

its wings! You could almost imagine it breathing fire! Or maybe there was no fire, but just a cloud from the pterosaur's mouth that came from its warm breath in the cold air. Have you ever seen your breath on a cold day? Most people did not believe that the dragon-like dinosaurs really existed until they started finding their big bones in England during the 1800s.

The dinosaur Spinosaurus also looked like a dragon with its long jaws and the huge wing-type "sail" on its back. Scientists believe that several of the dinosaurs, including Ouranosaurus, Rebbachisaurus, and Amargasaurus, had this same type of sail. They also believe that the "sail" on the reptile Dimetrodon was similar to the dinosaurs' sail, and that this was a type of heat regulator for all of them. If they became too hot, they turned their backs to the sun. If they became too cold, they turned their sides toward the sun to let their "sails" absorb all that heat.

Look and Learn

Soon after the dinosaur discoveries were made, **museums** or showcases for the dinosaurs started popping up all over the place. If you were going to make your own museum, what would you do? You can make your own museum or display by using a package of plastic dinosaurs from a toy store, several shoeboxes, and a batch of play dough. To make the play dough you need the following ingredients:

1¼ cups of flour
½ cup of salt
1 envelope of powdered unsweetened drink mix
2½ tablespoons of cooking oil
¾ cup of warm water

Fun Fact

Hot, Cold, or Just Right?

The most obvious way to find out a person's temperature is to use a thermometer. But there are other ways to figure out whether a person is warm or cold. One way to tell when a human is too hot is if he or she starts sweating. A person who is too cold will shiver or have "goose bumps." Have you ever worn a mood ring? The ring will change colors depending on the body temperature of the person who is wearing it.

With an adult's help, measure the ingredients and stir them together. Then knead the dough for a little while. This dough will keep well in a sealed container, or will dry hard if it is left out in the air.

Once you have your play dough ready, all you have to do is set up your boxes to be the different rooms of your museum, and decide where each dinosaur will be displayed. Then put enough play dough in each spot to hold the dinosaur in place. Once the playdough dries, your museum will remain just the way you designed it. Now you have your own shoe-box museum!

Hidden Hints

Paleontologists and **geologists** work together to decide how old rocks and dinosaurs are. Certain dinosaur fossils are found in a definite age or layer of rock. Rocks from one time period will have only certain dinosaur fossils in it. Some rocks contain particular types of chemicals. The geologists can measure the amount of these chemicals as a way of measuring the age of the rocks. When a certain amount of the chemical is gone, a set amount of time has passed.

The layers of rock help us to know how old the fossils are and where the fossils are located. They also tell us how old the rocks are by the different types and sizes of the layers of rock such as sandstone and limestone. For those reasons, most scientists today have a pretty good idea of where the dinosaurs could or should be. The land is continually moving, though, so dinosaur hunters sometimes still are surprised when they find a dinosaur in an unexpected place. One problem that scientists have run into is that when the continents started moving, the mountains pushed up, turning some of

Words to Know

museum:
A museum is a place where different things are stored and displayed for others to see and study. Many dinosaurs fossils are on display in museums all over the world.

Words to Know

geologist:
A geologist is someone who works in the field of geology, which is another word for the study of the earth. Many geologists study rocks and the history of our planet.

the layers of rock completely over, so that what might now appear to be a layer from a certain time actually may be from another.

You can see these layers in a canyon. Years ago, people panned for gold in canyons hoping to find a treasure. What they hadn't planned on finding was a different kind of treasure: dinosaur bones. Imagine looking up and seeing a huge bone sticking out of a rock wall! Stranger discoveries have been made.

The First Discovery

What would you think if you had never heard of a dinosaur and you found an enormous bone in your backyard? Not long after America was settled, a man found what he thought was part of a giant human. In fact, it turned out to be a bone from the meat-eater Megalosaurus! This bone was the first of its kind to be named dinosaur, which means "great lizard." For centuries, any dinosaur that looked like it could have or would have eaten meat was called a Megalosaurus. This type of dinosaur would never have had to go to the dentist, because it always had new teeth waiting to replace any teeth that were lost or harmed.

After Megalosaurus, the next dinosaur to be given a scientific name was Iguanodon, which means "iguana tooth." Imagine sifting through a pile of rocks and finding a giant tooth! This happened one day to Dr. Gideon Mantell's wife. It was found in the southern part of England, which remains a prime hunting ground for dinosaur fossils to this day. Later when she showed it to her husband, he thought that it resembled a modern-day iguana's tooth.

Which One?

You might be shocked if you saw my enormous antlers. You might also have thought that I would like St. Patrick's Day. Which one am I?

A. Stag-Moose
B. Steppe Bison
C. Eastern Elk
D. Irish Elk

D. Irish Elk

Dino Discovery

Use the scientist's notebook and decoder to learn of an amazing discovery!

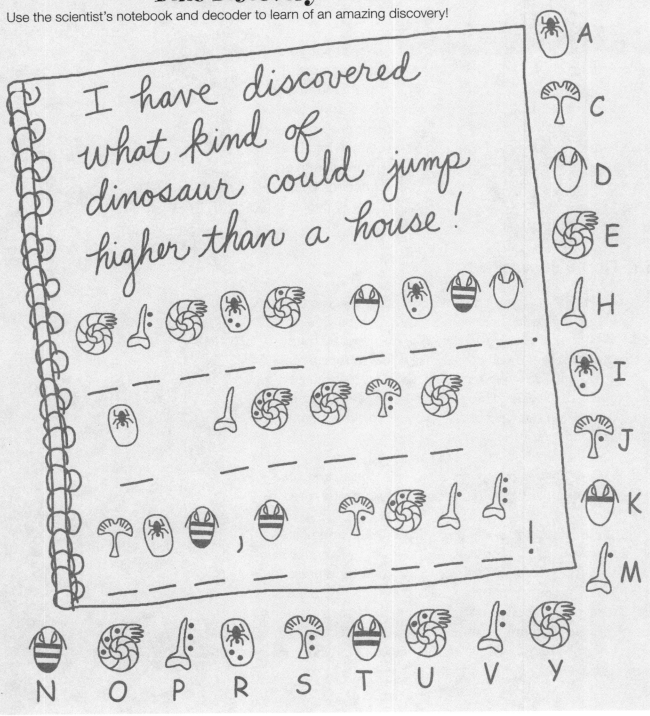

He also discovered another chunk of a fossil with a sharp spike that he believed was part of the dinosaur's nose. Thirty skeletons similar to the Iguanodon's then were found in a coal mine in Belgium, and scientists could tell from looking at them that the spike Dr. Mantell thought was a nose was actually more like a thumb. Before this mistake had been straightened out, a sculpture, bearing the horn or spike-like nose, had been created in Crystal Park in London. This life-size model is large enough to hold more than 20 people at a time, and is still on display today.

Whose Thumbprint?

An Iguanodon probably left behind a fairly large thumb-print. How big do you think those giant thumbs were in comparison to yours? If you want to see how big your thumbprint is, you can find out by making a batch of thumbprint cookies.

You will need to have an adult help you make these cookies. You also will need a roll of ready-to-bake sugar cookie dough from the grocery store's refrigerated section, and a cookie sheet.

1. Coat the cookie sheet with cooking spray and set the oven to the temperature that's given in the directions on the package of cookie dough.
2. Roll the dough into golf-ball-sized balls and place them on the cookie sheet.
3. Dip your thumb into white sugar and then press it once into each ball.
4. Ask an adult to bake the cookies for you, according to the directions on the package.

Who am I?

If you wrote out the beginning of my name, you probably would want to put a knife, a fork, a spoon, and a glass with me.
Who am I?

Plateosaurus

Can you still see your prints after the cookies are baked? If you want to make the cookies look more like the Iguanodon's thumb and claw, sink a chocolate kiss in the cookies after they come out of the oven!

Fun Fact

Home Sweet Bone
There were so many dinosaur bones found in one place in Wyoming that a shepherd built a cabin out of them. The place eventually became known as Bone Cabin Quarry!

How did the dinosaurs know we were coming?

Bronto saw us!

TODAY'S SPECIAL
BEEF $ 1.99/lb.

Chapter 7

The Hunt Begins

What Are the Odds?

You might think that finding a dinosaur would be unusual, but as you learned in the last chapter, even people who live in the United States have found dinosaur bones. The reason that most people don't see them is that the bone-filled land is covered with grass and trees. If you want to go on your own dinosaur fossil hunt, you will need an adult to go with you. Limestone pits or the banks of rivers are good places to search. If nothing else, you may find old bottles, arrowheads, or polished rocks carried there by floods. Although most dinosaur hunters thought the odds were against them, plenty of skeletons have been found.

Who am I?

I was named for my different kinds of teeth. All three kinds of them are similar to the teeth of many kinds of mammals of today.
Who am I?

Heterodontosaurus

The Hunters

In the 1800s, the Gold Rush in California made a lot of people start digging in the mountains. While they were hunting for their treasure, they stumbled across entire fossilized skeletons. Railroad and bridge builders also found dinosaur bones in other states. Soon, several fossil hunters were competing with each other to see who could find the biggest, the most unusual, and the greatest number of dinosaur bones. When the area known as the Morrison Formation was discovered, there was probably as much excitement among the fossil hunters

as there had been when gold was discovered in California. This area, which was filled with dinosaur fossils, stretched from Canada almost to the Mexican border. It was as large as the state of Texas. This discovery occurred during what was called the "Bone Wars," and it increased the rivalry or competition between two of the most well-known fossil hunters, Edward Cope and Othniel Marsh. Because of these battles, they discovered many new dinosaurs, but their disagreements and deliberate trickery also led to misnaming, renaming, and even the destruction of some of the **specimens**.

As people started traveling to more remote or distant spots in the 1900s, they found that dinosaur fossils were scattered all over the world. Some were even in Antarctica, in South America, and areas of Asia. You would think that because people have been searching for so many years, there wouldn't be any new discoveries to make, but paleontologists and geologists (and amateur fossil hunters just like you) keep finding new varieties of dinosaurs every year.

When new fossils were discovered in Tanzania during the 1900s, more than 200 tons of fossils were dug up, hand-carried by workers to ships, and sent thousands of miles away to museums.

It certainly would have been easier on these workers if they had been carrying bones that had been turned into Amazing Bones! To make an Amazing Bone, all you need is a chicken bone left over from dinner. Clean it well and place it in a clear jar filled with one cup of vinegar. Check the bone each day for a week and see what happens!

What Is the Cost?

Do you think that the people who were living in the late 1800s wondered what was wrong with the fossil hunters? Why were they willing to spend so much time and money to

Words to Know

specimens:
Specimens are samples of something. If you wanted to know how a whole batch of cookies turned out, you could sample one cookie; that cookie would be a specimen. Dinosaur bones are specimens used to learn about the dinosaurs.

Who am I?

On each hand I had five fingers. On each foot I had three toes. I am probably just the opposite of what you would think of as a dinosaur who was all wet.
Who am I?

Dryosaurus

Keep Looking

Can you find the one and only time in the letter grid that the word FOSSIL is spelled correctly? The answer might be side to side, top to bottom, diagonal, or backward! Use a marker to color in the boxes where the word FOSSIL is found.

Q	O	Q	Q	T	P	K	I	E
T	K	S	E	E	P	S	E	Q
K	T	Q	S	K	S	T	Q	P
E	Q	P	K	O	T	K	P	P
T	Q	K	L	F	O	E	Q	E
I	L	F	O	S	L	L	I	L
Q	E	P	O	O	I	K	T	T
F	F	O	S	S	S	I	L	O
P	E	Q	F	S	S	T	Q	Q
F	O	S	S	I	O	F	O	S
Q	E	P	I	L	F	P	Q	E
L	I	S	S	F	O	S	S	I
E	Q	P	S	O	S	E	Q	P
O	S	F	O	S	S	L	I	F
T	D	Q	F	S	I	K	T	Q
E	Q	P	T	I	K	Q	K	K

EXTRA FUN: Use the same marker to fill in ALL the boxes where the letters F-O-S-S-I-L are found. What have you uncovered?

save a few bones? People must have wondered if most of these men and their sponsors (the people who supported them) were interested in history and science. There were also many buyers anxiously awaiting these one-of-a-kind treasures. Were the fossil hunters more interested in making a profit?

What would you do if you found a dinosaur skeleton? Would you try to sell it? There are some people who buy dinosaur bones, but the price is not as high as you might think it would be. You might guess that they would be worth millions of dollars, but some people are only willing to pay a few thousand, even for a nearly complete dinosaur.

Wrapping It Up

You might think that finding the bones would be the hardest part of fossil hunting, but usually the biggest problem is shipping them safely from one place to another. The buyers of these fossils often live far from the place where the fossils are found. Many of the early fossils were destroyed because, just like your bones, they can break. Oddly enough, these bones were prepared for their trip in much the same way that the doctor would protect your bones if they had been broken. Both the doctors and the dinosaur hunters use plaster of Paris, a powder that becomes hard after you add water to it. The doctor doesn't want this to stick to your skin, so he wraps your leg with cloth to protect it.

The Hunt Begins

The fossil hunters used to use paper to wrap the bones, but now they use a clear plastic next to the bone. The plaster cast then goes on top of the protective layer. When the bone reaches its new home, the process is reversed to remove the cast. Sometimes the fossil hunters only **excavate** one-half of the bone, leaving some stone around the fossil to protect its underside. Recently doctors have started using air-filled supports for temporary casts. Do you think today's fossil hunters do the same thing?

The Job Is Just Starting

As you can see, there are many jobs associated with fossil hunting. How many jobs can you name that could help people see the dinosaur treasures? What about paleontologists, museum curators, geologists, park rangers, artists, and structural engineers who build the exhibits? You probably didn't know that they need explosives experts, too. One dinosaur was found with just its tail sticking out of a mountain! Rather than using hammers, chisels, or some type of knife to dig out the bones, these fossil hunters had to very carefully use explosives and then find a way to haul tons of rock away from the site! Do you think that they may have accidentally destroyed many

Words to Know

excavate:
When you excavate something, you remove it from somewhere. The dinosaurs' bones are usually excavated from the ground. Sometimes they are found under the water or layers of rock.

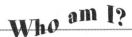
Who am I?

By my name, you might think I was related to a hawk or other birds of prey. I had extremely sharp claws and a long neck. I may have been small compared to a lot of the dinosaurs, but I was a big hunter.
Who am I?

Velociraptor

Which One?

I could never have been accused of wearing a long face. I would never have been able to "bear" it if someone called me small, because I was just the opposite. Which one am I?

A. Woolly Mammoth
B. Yesterday's Camel
C. Lesser Bilby
D. Giant Short-faced Bear

D. Giant Short-faced Bear

of the specimens with these methods? Once the paleontologists excavate enough to see the outline of the bone, they use delicate instruments like dental tools, an ear syringe, a paintbrush, a tape measure, and an awl to finish uncovering the bones.

Your Own Excavation

If you want to see what it is like to go on an excavation, all you have to do is take a half gallon of vanilla ice cream, place it in a large bowl, and allow it to thaw just a little, until it is soft enough to stir. Mix a package of gumballs into the soft ice cream, and then scoop it into foam cups and refreeze it. When the ice cream becomes hard again, you and your friends or your family can try digging out or excavating the gumballs while trying not to disturb the ice cream. When you think you have found all the gumballs, it's time to eat the ice cream, too!

The Hunted

Would you like to find a fossil? First, you need to know what they look like, so you might try searching through an encyclopedia or going on the Internet. Then you have to decide what type of fossil you are interested in finding. There are lots of things that different scientists call fossils, including the frozen mammoths that they have discovered in the Arctic, the animals buried in asphalt in the La Brea tar pits in California, and even the tiny white specks in the black rocks in your driveway, called rice agate. Some fossils are called prints. When an animal that was trapped in a lava flow eventually decayed, it left a perfect mold of its body in the hardened lava rock. Or, a leaf

Flying Fossil

Seems like there is only half of this dragonfly fossil. Can you help the scientists get a more complete look at this discovery? Draw the other half of the dragonfly, copying the first half square by square into the empty side of the grid.

Did you get to see the **WIZTLMUOB**?

Yes! I also saw the **WRML HLZI**!

EXTRA FUN: Use a reverse substitution code (A=Z, B=Y, etc.) to see what these silly scientists are saying to each other.

Fun Fact

New Again

Many animals grow new teeth to replace their old ones the same way the dinosaurs did. Other animals grow new parts. Starfish can grow new arms and a new body, even if there is only a small part of the center of the body left.

What kind of dinosaur can you ride in a rodeo?

A Bronco-saurus!

may have fallen onto some sand and then become covered by more sand that was eventually compressed enough so that it turned into rock, known as sedimentary rock.

You can make your own leafprint fossil. With an adult's help, follow these steps:

1. Mix ½ cup of plaster of Paris with ¼ cup of water in a disposable cup.
2. Add a drop of food coloring and mix it in. Then pour the soupy plaster onto a plastic bag.
3. As the plaster begins to harden, lay your leaf on the top of the plaster and press on it very gently.
4. When the plaster sets up hard, pull the leaf off to reveal your fossil print.

You can do the same thing by placing a plastic dinosaur or dog bone halfway into a circle of plaster as it begins to dry. When you are through, be sure to throw away the cup and bag.

Rocks and Fossils

You might find some dinosaur bones or other kind of fossils as you learn more about rocks, because fossils are only found in certain kinds of rocks. You might think that all rocks look alike and that they were formed at the same time or in the same way, but that's not true.

As you learned in an earlier chapter of this book, the Triassic Period was named after the three layers of sedimentary rock that were deposited during that time—sandstone, mudstone, and shale—so you would expect to find dinosaurs from that era in those kinds of rocks. Don't expect to find many dinosaur fossils that survived, though, because the Triassic Period was around 230 million years ago. You also already know that the Jurassic Period was named after the Jura Mountains in Europe. Scientists can tell when these mountains were formed, and they classify all the rocks and dinosaurs that they think came from that era as Jurassic. The name Cretaceous comes from the layers of chalk, a soft form of limestone, that was formed millions of years ago when sea creatures and certain minerals sank to the bottom of the ocean and formed sediment. So just keep looking. Scientists find many of the dinosaur fossils from these periods, and so can you!

Would you like to make your own chalk? You won't need any sea creatures to make it. All you will need is a little help from an adult, some plaster of Paris, and a few supplies that you will have at home:

1. Line an empty toilet paper roll with a piece of waxed paper.
2. Cover the bottom of the tube with a large piece of tape to keep the plaster of Paris from leaking out.
3. Mix 1 cup of plaster of Paris with about 1/3 cup of water and a drop or two of your favorite food coloring in a foam cup.
4. Stir the plaster until it is like pudding and then pour it into the tube, filling it to the top.

It will take about an hour or so for the chalk to harden. Then all you have to do is rip off the paper roll and the waxed paper, and you are ready to draw.

Finding the Bones

Some of the earliest discoveries of dinosaurs were made along the coast of England. Dinosaurs are still being uncovered there as the tides continue to wash the soil away.

Which One?

You might have expected me to come out right before the sun went down, or to see me flying over the ocean. My last name is the same as a common bird seen today. Which one am I?

A. Labrador Duck
B. Dusky Seaside Sparrow
C. Guam Flycatcher
D. Night Heron

B. Dusky Seaside Sparrow

Why didn't the dinosaur cross the road?

There weren't any roads then!

Try This

Mud Painting

You could use real mud to paint a picture on your sidewalk and then hose it away, or you could use a batch of instant chocolate pudding and paint your picture with your fingers on a cookie sheet or plate. The best part of painting with pudding is that you can eat it, too!

Dinosaur bones also can be uncovered in the middle of a continent, where the wind has removed the sand that covered the bones. At Dinosaur National Monument in Utah, which is located in the Morrison Formation, fossils of these ancient creatures can still be seen throughout the park and in a rock wall located right in the visitors' center. You may wonder why so many of these fossils are in the same place. Whole skeletons of dinosaurs frequently are found in mass graves. Scientists look at these "dinosaur graveyards" and wonder if they all died together in some natural disaster the way that the buffalo or cattle did in the early American West. Confused buffalo would accidentally run off of the cliffs in a rainstorm, or sometimes they would become trapped in a valley when a rainstorm came and filled it with mud. Could something like this have happened to the dinosaurs too?

Host a Bone Hunt

Who knows? Maybe the bone that was buried and then forgotten by your dog will be dug up someday and become someone else's fossil find! Even though you're not a dog, you can have your own bone hunt using bones made out of Popsicle sticks. Count the number of people, and then get out four or five sticks per person so that everyone can be looking for the same number of bones. Next, put a piece of masking tape on each stick with a number between 1 and 10. Then have someone hide the bones around the house. Tell everyone how many bones they must find. When each person has found his or her limit, they should wait for the rest of the players to find theirs. Then,

everyone adds up the numbers on their bones to see who has the highest total number.

Certain Animals in Certain Places

When the mountains were formed and the continents were drifting apart, the dinosaurs were separated from each other as though they had been placed on islands. Many scientists believe this is why so many new species of dinosaurs appeared in the Cretaceous period. They evolved to fit their new surroundings, and many of them could only be found in certain places. For example, most of the horned dinosaurs were found in areas above the equator. Even today, several types of animals can only be found in certain places, or in certain **climates**. The opossum lives in the United States, while the panda munches bamboo in China, and penguins live on the ice in Antarctica. The only way we can actually see so many of them is by bringing them from their natural home to a zoo.

Dinosaurs on Display

Just think if you were the museum director who received all those crates from Tanzania! How would you know how all of the bones went back together? How can any scientist be sure that she is setting up a skeleton in the right way? When paleontologists are lucky, they keep finding more and more of the same fossil skeletons. But many times, all they have to work with when they attempt to identify a new species is a single, broken bone. Even if they do have a full skeleton, it's only like an outline. How did they know how much it weighed? Usually, they use similar modern-day animals as an example of what they think it should look like.

Who am I?

I am the most famous of all the extinct birds. My name rhymes with a toy on a string. One of my biggest problems was that I was a flightless bird living on an island. I disappeared from the earth more than 300 years ago.
Who am I?

Dodo

Words to Know

climate:
The climate of an area is a description of what the weather is like there. The climate that the dinosaurs lived in changed from place to place and from year to year. Sometimes the climate was hot and dry; other times it was wet and cold.

Which One?

The largest of all of the sharks, I really made a splash when I hit the water. I am also a "mega" hit in most shark books. Which one am I?

A. Big Thicket Hog-nosed Skunk
B. Megalodon
C. Blue Pike
D. Crow Shark

B. Megalodon

Comparing dinosaurs to modern animals worked in the case of the Apatosaurus. Its neck looks almost exactly like the neck of a turkey. Unfortunately, this idea didn't work for Elasmosaurus, which was one of the plesiosaurs; the fossil hunter thought its long neck was its tail and put it together with its neck upside down! Do you think that you would be good at putting fossils back together? One test you could do is to try placing several pictures of dinosaurs upside down on a table. Without turning them around, can you guess what they are? Try holding the pictures up to a mirror. Now what do you see? Can your friends guess which ones they are by doing the same tests?

All Mixed Up

What would you think if you went into a people display at the museum and a dinosaur paleontologist had put the head of a gorilla on a human's body? Something like that happened to the Apatosaurus. Museum directors placed another dinosaur's head on its body and left it that way for many years. Things like this often happen when paleontologists only find parts of several different skeletons, and have to figure out how they go together. Fossil hunters don't usually even find complete dinosaur skulls because the bone that their skulls were made of is very thin. The skulls often break because of the enormous weight of the rocks pressing down on them.

Because scientists believed that Diplodocus dragged its tail on the ground, they displayed it that way in numerous museums. Later they

Why don't dinosaurs ever forget?

Can you find the seven words that make up
the answer to this riddle?

Who am I?

I am one of the first dinosaurs found that was thought to have possibly had feathers. Although my feathers were never found, the idea of a feathered dinosaur took flight from me.

Who am I?

Avimimus

Words to Know

reconstruct:

When you reconstruct something, you rebuild it. When the fossil hunters find the many broken pieces of dinosaurs, they take them to museums, where workers put them back together or reconstruct them.

decided that it actually used its tail to balance itself by holding it up in the air! They also had a difficult time trying to decide whether Iguanodon stood on all four feet or only two. For many years, museum directors thought he rested his body on his tail like a kangaroo until they tried to place his skeleton on display. Then they realized that they would have to break his tail to rest it in that position!

Many people often go to natural history museums to see dinosaurs. If you want to find a museum that is close to your area, try looking for one on the Internet or in your phone book. Another place you could visit is a children's museum. Many children's museums offer activities about dinosaurs, and some even display exhibits that include dinosaur robots.

Which Bone Is Which?

If you've seen one bone you've seen them all, right? Well, not exactly. A rib bone is small, while a thighbone is large. The same was true with the dinosaurs. Of course, if you found the thighbone of a very small dinosaur, you might think it was a bone from the lower leg of a large dinosaur. If you want to quiz your family or friends, you can play the Bone Guessing Game. The next time you have fried chicken, save some bones from the wings and the thighs, and a few from the breast. Then wash and dry the bones. See if your family can guess which bone was a wing bone, a breastbone, or a thigh bone.

Another activity that would be fun to try is to **reconstruct** a skeleton. All you need is a whole chicken from your grocery store. First you will have to ask an adult to cook the chicken until the meat falls off the bones. Once the bones are washed (they will probably break during cooking and washing), you can try to rebuild the chicken's original skeleton. If you need help, you can try looking up pictures of a skeleton in a book or on the Internet.

Chapter 8

Ever Changing

Crazy Crocodiles

Archosaurs, known as the "ruling reptiles," were divided into three groups: the crocodiles, the dinosaurs, and the pterosaurs. Scientists believe that the crocodile evolved from an animal that lived in the water; into one that climbed onto the land and eventually returned to live in the water again. Some believe that the dinosaurs also evolved from a crocodile-like reptile. Many of the dinosaurs, including Baryonyx, Spinosaurus, and Suchomimus (whose name means "crocodile mimic"), have the long, toothy jaws of the crocodiles. Several types of dinosaurs, such as Ceratosaurus, had a tail that would have propelled them through the water easily. While most scientists don't believe that dinosaurs lived in the water, they do believe that many of them swam very well when they needed to escape predators or wanted to search for food along the shore.

In the Cretaceous period, some of the crocodiles, such as Deinosuchus and Sarcosuchus, were between 40 and 50 feet long! Some experts think that they ate dinosaurs. Do you think they could have eaten a T. rex?

Who am I?

The beginning of my name sounds like I lived out in the ocean, but actually I lived on land. Because I was so big, when they first found my bones they thought I was a whale.

Who am I?

Cetiosaurus

Long after the crocodiles were the **survivors** in the swamps and rivers all over the rest of the world, the South Pole was home for a salamander the size of a horse. This area wasn't as cold then as it is today, and seemed to be a haven for animals that had disappeared from every other location in the ancient world.

You can hold your own survivor contest by challenging your family or friends to see who can set the fastest time by going through your own survivor course. What kind of obstacles can you make? How about stepping into the middle of several tires, crawling through a bunch of boxes, wading through a pool, and then untying a flag when you reach the end of the course?

You're Wrestling What?

The crocodiles of today are a much smaller version of the animal that you would have seen in the time of the dinosaurs. Alligators also belong to the same family as the crocodiles. Alligators have tremendous strength in their jaws, especially when they are snapping them shut, but their trainers know how to use their hands to hold the alligator's mouth closed. Crocodiles are much larger and more vicious than the alligators. Have you ever watched a show where someone wrestles with an alligator? Can you imagine anyone training or wrestling with the crocodiles? How about their ancestors or their cousin, the dinosaur?

A Rocky Croc

If the dinosaurs were still around, someone would probably be trying to train them or at least display them in a cage. Maybe the safest kind of crocodile that you could have would be one that was made out of rock! If you want to make one,

Words to Know

survivor:
A survivor is one who succeeds in lasting a long time. The dinosaurs survived for millions of years on an ever-changing planet.

Which One?

You might expect to hear me say "moo." Or you may think that I live way out in the ocean. My first name sounds like it has something to do with the stars. Which one am I?

   A. Steller's Sea Cow
   B. Crow Shark
   C. Big Thicket Hog-nosed Skunk
   D. Blue Pike

A. Steller's Sea Cow

all you need is some glue, a piece of cardboard, and several rocks. You need to pick out three oval-shaped rocks, one of them larger than the other two; six small round rocks; and three pointed ones, one medium-sized and two small. Once you've gathered your rocks, here's how to put your crocodile together:

1. Lay the largest oval rock down on your piece of cardboard. This rock will be the crocodile's body.
2. Set the other two oval rocks at one end of the body to make the jaws of the crocodile. To keep the jaws slightly open, place the two small pointed rocks between the jaws, toward the back, and glue them all together.

What do you call a dinosaur wearing a blindfold?

Doyouthinkysarus!

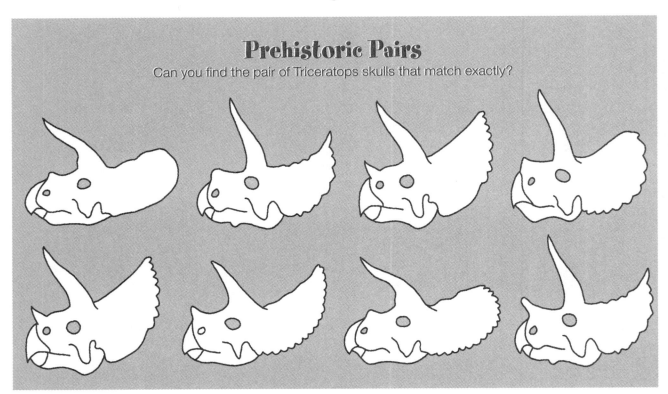

Prehistoric Pairs

Can you find the pair of Triceratops skulls that match exactly?

3. Tape the jaws till the glue sets, then glue two of the small round rocks on top of the jaw for eyes, and the other four around the body for legs.
4. Now glue the last pointed rock to the end of the crocodile to make its tail.

When your crocodile is completely dry, you can paint it and add all kinds of decorations.

Which Is the Best Way to Go?

If you were going to classify dinosaurs or crocodiles as the scientists do, where would you start? Would you sort them by the type of mouth or beak that they had, or the variety, number, or size of their teeth? Would you look at what kind of skin they had covering their bodies, or would you look at their feet and legs? If you sorted them by their legs, would you measure their length, or how they used them, or would you just start by counting how many they used to walk around?

Scientists who have studied the dinosaurs have decided that the number of legs the dinosaurs used varied based on which type of dinosaur it was and the period of time in which it lived. Some of the dinosaurs seemed to prefer walking on two legs, while other dinosaurs eventually chose to walk on all four. How do we know this? In several places throughout the world, they left their footprints as a permanent record. Scientists can tell from these records how big the dinosaurs were, whether they ran on two or four feet, and how fast they ran. These prints make them think that the sauropods only ran at a speed of about four miles an hour, while some meat-eaters could reach speeds of more than thirty miles an hour!

Who am I?

The only things longer than my front legs were my long neck and tail. My name sounds like the opposite of a front-iosaurus.
Who am I?

Brachiosaurus

A two-ton Tyrannosaurus tried to teach Thomas to tie his shoes. How many "Ts" in that?

There are 2 "Ts" in "ThaT"!

Why Did the Dinosaur Cross the Road?

Find the correct path for this dinosaur from START to END. Pick up letters along the way that will spell the answer to this riddle.

It's a Matter of Survival

There are many reasons why the dinosaurs survived for as long as they did. Some scientists say three things that really helped are that they had a tail for balancing themselves, their bones were light because they were hollow, and they developed a different shape of hipbone that helped them to walk upright. The meat-eaters fared well because they used their back legs for running and used their front legs to hold on to their food. All of these meat-eaters could stand upright, which helped them to be able to run faster, unlike the early plant-eaters whose larger stomachs eventually forced them to use four legs to support all that weight. Eventually, the plant-eaters **adapted** to the conditions around them by developing stronger teeth and standing on two legs again.

The Iguanodon could run on two or four legs. Psittacosaurus, known as the "parrot reptile," was one of the first horned dinosaurs, and scientists think it may have used all four feet. Triceratops was like our rhinoceros and hippopotamus and always walked on four feet. As time went on, the dinosaurs' toes decreased in number and many of their toes evolved into hooves found on all four of their feet!

If you want to see how it would feel to walk like a dinosaur, you can hold a tiptoe relay race, which is like a regular relay race except that everyone on both teams can only walk on their tiptoes. Another way to play this game is to have everyone race using only their heels like Iguanadon hooves.

Words to Know

adapted:
When something changes to fit its surroundings or environment, we say it has adapted. The dinosaurs changed and adapted for millions of years before they vanished.

Who am I?

Although I should be worth more than a penny to a collector, by the sound of my name you might think that was all I was worth.
Who am I?

Centrosaurus

Try This

Hairy or Fuzzy Dinosaurs

You can make your own fuzzy or hairy dinosaurs from a package of chenille craft wires. The dinosaur's body can be formed using circles of wire, and then you can attach other wires for legs and a head. To make the dinosaur's neck, you can wrap the wire around a pencil or the end of a spoon and then gently slide the coiled wire off.

Sitting Down on the Job

Why do animals choose to "sit up" on their back legs? You see animals do this all the time. Raccoons, squirrels, and rabbits nibble their food while holding it with their front paws. Cats will sit on their hind legs when they play with a string dangled in front of them. Dogs "sit up" to beg for their food. Some animals, such as circus horses, bears, and elephants, can even be taught to walk around on their hind legs, but it isn't their natural position and they quickly drop back to all fours.

Kangaroos, unlike other animals, seem to be sitting up all the time. Some people say they are boxing. Can you think of any other animal that sits up all of the time? What about some animals that never "sit up," like cows or pigs? Humans like to crawl first, and then they pull themselves to a sitting position before they decide that they are ready to walk. How long can you or your friends sit in one place? How long can you last if you put your back against a wall and pretend you are sitting on a chair?

It's a Fact

Why don't we all have paws like cats, dogs, and raccoons? Evolution may have something to with that, too! You would never even know that cats have claws until they feel they need them. Dogs and people have nails instead of claws. Do horses, cows, and deer have hooves because their nails and claws would wear out too fast? All these things—nails, claws, and hooves—are made of a substance called keratin. So is the hair on your head.

Fun with Your Feet

Have you ever really looked at your feet? You probably think that all feet look alike. If you were to compare them, though, you might be surprised. To check this out, gather a few of your friends and family and have everyone take off their shoes and socks to see the differences in people's toes. A lot of people think they have funny-looking feet. Some of you might notice that your feet look like your parents' feet, or that your middle toes are longer than your big toes! Some people complain that they really don't have a little toe at all.

Like the dinosaurs, many animals have four feet rather than two feet and two hands. Can you imagine trying to eat your food with your feet? You could try doing several things with your feet and toes, like writing, drawing, picking up pennies, or using a spoon. You also could try painting with your toes. Can you do the same things with either hand?

The Test of Time

Some people believe that after all this time, the only true relatives of the dinosaurs are the birds. Others think the reptiles are all that is left of the dinosaurs. Would the dinosaurs have stayed the same if they lived in a different time? Some people today are busy using their time to try to fix or save the planet. They also are using their time to look into the past as well as the future. Do you think the dinosaurs would have lived longer if they could have had someone trying to save their planet?

Which One?

You may know my descendants. Some of them are in rodeos, and others are on farms. I hope this clue will "steer" you in the right direction. Which one am I?

A. Irish Elk
B. Quagga
C. Arabian Gazelle
D. Auroch

D. Auroch

Which dinosaur was the Lone Ranger's sidekick?

Tontosaurus!

Fun Fact

What Color Was That Dinosaur?

Although the skins of several fossilized dinosaurs show different textures and patterns, the color of their skin is a mystery. The colors of the dinosaurs we see in pictures or movies today are only guesses of what their true color may have been.

Timing is important, and maybe that is why we are so fascinated by keeping track of time. We measure time by the second, the hour, the day, and the year. One way to measure time is with a stopwatch or a clock. Have you ever timed how long it takes you to get ready for school or make your bed? Or how long it takes for you eat lunch or walk the dog? These time measurements are just for fun, but there are occasions when you need to measure time; for example, when you are cooking. How did people know how long to cook a hard-boiled egg before there were any clocks? An early invention that was used to tell time was called an hourglass. Smaller ones were later made to measure minutes. To make your own minute glass you will need two empty 24-ounce pop bottles, a small metal washer, three cups of sand, and a roll of masking tape.

1. Pour the sand into one of the pop bottles.
2. Place the washer on top of that bottle's opening.
3. Place the other bottle upside-down on the first one so the tops of the pop bottles are together, and fasten them with masking tape.
4. Turn the bottles over and time how long it takes for the sand to run from the top bottle into the bottom one. It should take one minute. If it's not accurate, you can unfasten the tape and add or take away sand until you have it right.

Once your timer is ready, you can use it when you need to keep track of the time when you are playing games. Use larger bottles and add more sand if you want to measure a longer amount of time.

End of the Story

Use the numbered clues to fill in the spaces along the dinosaur's body, placing one letter in each space. The last letter of one word is the first letter of the next.

When you are finished, write the spotted letters on the lines to get the riddle's answer.

1. Garbage
2. Really big
3. Opposite of GOOD
4. One who doesn't tell the truth
5. Rodent that looks like a huge mouse
6. Outfit worn in ancient Greece that looks like a sheet
7. One more time
8. It is hammered
9. Opposite of MORE

What came after the dinosaurs?

_ _ _ _ _
_ _ _ _ _ !

The Tail End

Tails were very important to the dinosaurs. One known as Opisthocoelicaudia is thought to have used its tail as a third limb, like the kangaroo. Scientists think that it balanced on its tail as it ate leaves from the tops of trees. Diplodocus' long tail may have been used to strike his enemies (on purpose or by accident) if he moved it quickly. The smaller Velociraptor might have propped itself up with its tail when it used its terrible claw located on its rear leg to protect itself from its enemies. Other dinosaurs may have used their tails to curl up and go to sleep like a dog or a cat.

The Tale of the Tail

All of these dinosaurs had tails, and so do most of the other creatures in the animal kingdom. What animals, other than humans, can you think of that don't have long tails? What do you think it would be like to try to wear a tail around all day? One way to find out is to try it. Sound simple? First you would have to decide if you want it to hang down like a cow's tail or stick up in the air like a poodle's. Clothes would definitely be a problem and where would you put your tail if you wanted to sit down? Imagine having a tail like a peacock; it would be like wearing a bride's dress or trying to fold up a fan all day long. You will want to think about what difficulties you would have, depending on which type of tail you choose. Then you need to figure out how to make that tail. You can make a tail out of things you have around the house: ribbons, ties, belts, feather dusters, and so forth. See if your friends want to make their own tails, too. Fasten them on and try to guess which animal each person is trying to be. See who can stand to wear his or her tail for the longest time.

How can you tell
a male dinosaur from
a female dinosaur?

Ask it a question.
If he answers,
it's a male;
if she answers,
it's female.

The Mystery

Who am I?

To hear my name you might think that I was part of a set or that there were two of me, but I am not twins; I was only one dinosaur with a wing-shaped crest on my head.

Who am I?

Parasaurolophus

What Do You Wonder About?

Dinosaurs are just one of the great mysteries. There are many other puzzles we have discovered throughout the history of our world. We have been left with questions such as these: Who built Stonehenge in England? Who built the pyramids in Egypt and the huge statues on Easter Island? Even more mysterious is why those things were built. What famous mysteries do you wonder about? Do you think it would be dangerous to travel in the Bermuda Triangle? Did the city of Atlantis actually exist and then sink beneath the sea?

Were there really unicorns? How do we know that there weren't? It hasn't been all that long since we learned about the unbelievable dinosaurs and other very strange creatures that died in a very short period of time all those millions of years ago.

Over time, we have learned a great deal about the world and solved many mysteries, but do you think we will ever find the answer to the greatest riddle of the dinosaurs: What happened to them? Is it possible that we could do something to prevent a great extinction from happening again? Some people have spent their whole lives trying to solve this mystery—a mystery that may hold the key to our future.

Changing Skins

Have you ever been walking along and thought you saw a small snake lying in the grass, and then when you looked a little closer, you realized it was only the outer covering that the snake had outgrown and shed? We know that several other animals do the same thing. Lobsters and crabs worm their way out of their shells, chickens lose their feathers, and every year, millions of empty cicada shells are found still holding onto tree bark.

Many varieties of shellfish, birds, and insects lose their outer coverings. Do you think that different kinds of reptiles, other than the snakes, shed their skins? You might be surprised to learn that all reptiles shed their outside coverings. Can you imagine living in the ancient Jurassic jungle and accidentally stepping on an Allosaurus skin? You might have been able to use it as a very large shelter from the storms!

Ready, Set, Find It!

One way to have fun is to go on a Dinosaur Scavenger Hunt. So, what will you be hunting? Even though you probably won't be looking for dinosaur skins, you could look for some of the things that also existed back in the days of the dinosaurs, such as rocks, ferns, cattails, pine needles, palm leaves, and maybe a shell from some animal! You can start your scavenger hunt by making several copies of the same list of items, one for each person. Choose someone who is not playing the game to keep track of the time. Then give everyone up to fifteen minutes to search for these things. The winner is the one who can bring back the most items before the time is up.

Try This

Solve This One

Have you ever tried to write your own riddles? It can be fun. Here's one to get you started: What do you call a dinosaur that runs all day? An "Ankle oh sore is" (Ankylosaurus).

Fun Fact

Take It or Leave It

Many of the dinosaurs ate only leaves. Many humans eat leaves, too. Maybe you eat some of these leaves: cabbage, lettuce, spinach, parsley, celery, or artichoke.

The Search Goes On

Have you ever read stories that are called science fiction, or tales from out of this world? Lots of these stories are about people living on other planets or people from other planets living in our world. Science fiction is also frequently written about weird-looking creatures that ooze along the ground, breathe differently than we do, and have lots of sharp body parts that they use as protection or defense. What could have been stranger than some of the fossils that scientists have found? They prove that some pretty odd-looking beasts inhabited the earth long before we got here!

You could try writing your own science-fiction story, even one about strange-looking dinosaurs. All you need to start a story is an idea or a few words. Words like: "The day was just like any other day, until I turned the corner. I couldn't believe my eyes . . ." Think what it would have been like if we had been the first ones on the planet and then we all disappeared! Would T. rex or one of the longnecks be looking for our fossils? Would they be displaying them in some museum with our toes growing out of our skulls?

Science-fiction writers often seem to be able to see into or predict the future. Even if it is accidental, many of the things they write about eventually seem to come true. Writers wrote about people traveling to the moon decades before it happened. Almost a hundred years ago, H. G. Wells wrote about atomic energy and traveling in space. He also predicted traveling through time. Do you think you will ever see that occur?

There are ways that you can travel back in time, and you don't need a special machine to do it! Ask an adult if he or she would take you to visit a science museum, or a museum that has displays about the history of your area. Another way

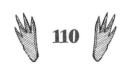

to visit yesterday is to go to an antique store. You will be amazed at how many of these antiques your family actually used not that long ago.

Where Did They Go?

Extinction is a natural process, like evolution, that lets the stronger animals survive. Scientists are always talking about "the great extinction" and trying to figure out what caused all the dinosaurs to die. What you probably don't know is that the famous extinction that occurred 65 million years

Space Traveler

Can you figure out which dinosaur is which, and which dinosaur is actually an alien? Use the following clues:

- The Toothosaur is not the one with three horns.
- Both the Tankopod and Flipodon have scales.
- The Sailosaur is next to the dinosaur with webbed feet.
- The Flipodon is not the one with spikes on its tail.

P.S. These are made-up dinosaur names!

Who am I?

I could have been nicknamed three-finger or long-foot, or I could have been called a lightweight. If I had feathers you might think that I look like a roadrunner.

Who am I?

Compsognathus

Words to Know

meteorite:
A meteorite is a part of a meteor from outer space that enters the earth's atmosphere. Several meteorites have hit the planet. Some people believe that a meteorite caused the extinction of the dinosaurs.

ago was not the first one. Research has shown that great numbers of animals have been wiped out at least two other times and maybe many more! About 250 million years ago, before the time of the dinosaurs, something caused most of the plants and animals that lived at that time to vanish from the earth. One common creature living at that time, the trilobite, has left numerous fossils everywhere. If you want to see what a small version of those creatures would look like today, try turning over a piece of rotting wood in your yard or dig into your garden. The sowbugs that will scatter in every direction look a lot like trilobites.

It appears that after many of the other animals died, the dinosaurs were allowed to develop and then expand their territory. Between the Triassic and Jurassic periods, a large sea developed between the north and south sections of Pangaea, and another period of extinction occurred that killed off the strong mammal-like reptiles. This allowed the dinosaurs to rule the land until the last great extinction 65 million years ago.

No Explanation for It

What do you think caused the mass extinction? No one seems to know for sure. Some scientists think that massive earthquakes or volcanoes occurred. Could volcanoes and the smoke from the fires they caused have kept the sun's rays from reaching Earth for months or even years? The animals that lived in the ocean or that were burrowed under the ground may have survived such conditions, but the plants and animals on land would need sunlight to survive.

Some scientists think a **meteorite** struck the planet, causing tidal waves, fires, or dust storms. There are enormous craters scattered all around the world, and one of them seems to have appeared 65 million years ago!

Edible Meteorites

What do you suppose that a meteorite might have looked like—a rough piece of rock, a big lump of iron, or a huge chunk of ice? To see your own Meteorite Masses, a kind of meteor that you can eat, you will need the help of an adult, a 9" × 13" cake pan, a 3-quart saucepan, and a few simple ingredients.

1. Coat the inside of the cake pan with butter.
2. Have the adult put 1 cup of sugar and 1 cup of corn syrup in the saucepan.
3. The adult should bring this mixture to a boil, and then remove it from the heat.
4. Stir in 1 cup of peanut butter; then add 1½ teaspoons of vanilla and 6½ cups of crispy rice cereal.
5. Pour the mixture into the cake pan. After it cools slightly, butter your hands and form the mixture into small "meteorites." Your Meteorite Masses will be ready to eat when they cool.

Fun Fact

X-Ray Vision

If you had x-ray vision, you could see through almost anything. Because people don't see this way, scientists use an x-ray machine to help them see inside the ancient dinosaur eggs they have found.

Gone Forever?

You've already learned that there still are ancient reptiles, the crocodiles and the turtles, living in our world today, while the most famous of them all, the dinosaur, has vanished. Did their watery homes or their ability to hibernate save many of the other reptiles that are still here? Many of them bury themselves to protect themselves from the heat.

Words to Know

descendants:
Your parent's descendants are their children (including you!) and their children's families. You are a descendant of your grandparents and parents. The dinosaurs also had descendants that they gave birth to.

Did the ancestors of these reptiles go underground until the danger, whatever it was, had passed?

Some people believe that the dinosaurs may still be here in the sense that they developed into our modern-day reptiles or birds. One reptile that many people think resembles a dinosaur is the Komodo dragon. This meat-eating lizard is around 10 feet long and weighs hundreds of pounds. Lizards come in all shapes and sizes, including the glass lizard, which looks like a snake; gila monsters, which look like a beaded salamander; iguanas; and the little geckoes, which have claws on their feet and sticky little barbed footpads that they use to scamper across your ceiling.

Some people wonder if many of today's mammals are **descendants** of the true dinosaurs, rather than the mammal-

Gotcha!

The letters in each column go in the squares directly below them, but not in the same order. Black squares are the spaces between words. When you have correctly filled in the grid, you will have the answer to this riddle:

Why did the Archaeopteryx catch the worm?

like reptiles. Elephants, hippopotamuses, and giraffes are very similar to the sauropods. Even the rhinoceros looks like a miniature Triceratops. Some of the hadrosaurs look very much like our cows, camels, horses, and goats.

Feathered Friends

In some ways it is possible to believe that birds are related to the dinosaur family. Archaeopteryx was a combination of a bird and a dinosaur that had teeth like a reptile, but his collarbones were joined together to form a wishbone, like the birds of today. Some of the dinosaurs that shared this trait were the Oviraptor, Velociraptor, and Tyrannosaurus rex. Do you know what and where your collarbones are? Most animals have them. They are the two bones that help attach your arms to the middle of your body, and they are found right under the collar of your shirt.

Many of the dinosaurs also had a ring of bones that supported their eye sockets. This type of support or protection is still found in many of the birds in the world today. Research shows that Archaeopteryx had wings, but that it didn't actually use them for flying. Archaeopteryx's wings had claws on them that it probably used to climb up into trees, then glide to the ground. The hoatzin, a bird that lives in South America today, also has claws on its wings, although it loses them after the first few weeks of its life. The hoatzin also climbs trees and then glides to the ground, especially if some animal is trying to catch it.

Did the Dinosaur Come Before the Chicken?

Why do you think all the birds come from eggs rather than by live birth? This could be another point that shows a link with egg-laying dinosaurs. An ostrich probably lays the

Fun Fact

Nice Tail!

Descendants of Archaeopteryx still had a tail, but all that remained of it was a small version of a tail called the pygostyle. The feathers were still were attached to it, just like the modern-day chickens and other birds. Try looking closely at your feathered friends when they come to eat at your bird feeder. Could they be related to dinosaurs?

Which One?

You may have wanted to saddle me up if you had seen me, but at a little over 2 feet tall, I was too small to ride. Which one am I?

A. Eohippus
B. Sloth Lemur
C. Bubal Hartebeest
D. Trilobite

A. Eohippus

 115

Try This

An Edible Nest You Can Make

Coat a plate with cooking spray. Then ask an adult to heat 6 ounces of almond bark for 1½ minutes in a clear glass bowl in a microwave oven. Add approximately 100 small stick pretzels, stir well, and put the mixture on the plate. Then shape the sticks into a nest using spoons. (This will keep you from burning your fingers.) The nest will become hard fairly quickly.

largest egg of any living bird, but the now-extinct elephant bird laid eggs that were reported to be more than a foot long and larger than any of the dinosaur eggs.

Do you suppose the dinosaurs roosted at night like chickens do? Most scientists no longer believe that a dinosaur could climb trees, but wouldn't it be scary to think that a T. rex could drop on you from a tree?

Dinosaurs were like birds in many ways. Some of them laid their eggs in nests made from sticks and mud. The ostrich has a gland that stores energy near its spinal column, and the Stegosaurus had a cavity in the same place. This gives some people another reason to believe that the two creatures were part of the same family. If you look at birds and then you look at pictures of dinosaurs, you may see what looks like a cockscomb on a chicken that is similar to the crested head on Corythosaurus.

Beaks and Mouths

Dinosaurs had several different kinds of mouths. There were duckbills, parrot-beaks, and many other varieties. The Oviraptors didn't have teeth, so they used their beaks to crush other dinosaur eggs in the same way that birds of today do to another bird's eggs. Some of the modern-day birds called raptors, such as the owls, eagles, and hawks, don't have teeth either; they use their sharp beaks and talons to catch their prey. How many types of bird beaks can you think of?

Birds have many uses for their beaks. Nuthatches use their beaks to crack nuts;

What Did One Fossil Say to the Other?

Answer as many clues below as you can, and write the letters into the grid. Work back and forth between the grid and clues until you discover the answer to the riddle.

Pi, opu nvdi dibohft gps nf!

A. Move like a dog's tail

___ ___ ___
1   25 26

B. An opening to let out air or water

___ ___ ___ ___
12 17 19 4

C. A place to live

___ ___ ___ ___ ___
2   21 22 28 27

D. Past tense of eat

___ ___ ___
11 15 7

E. To move gently back and forth

___ ___ ___ ___
5   8   3   20

F. Number after eight

___ ___ ___ ___
14 23 24 13

G. To reflect light

___ ___ ___ ___ ___
16 10 9   6   18

EXTRA FUN: To learn how the other fossil replies, substitute letters either one before or one after the letters shown.

117

Which One?

I was one of the few felines (cats) with such large dagger-like teeth. You would probably have thought I would meow or maybe even roar. Which one am I?

A. Bali Tiger
B. Cape Lion
C. Saber-toothed Cat
D. Lesser Bilby

C. Saber-toothed Cat

woodpeckers dig bugs out of old wood; and pelicans carry fish in their beaks even when they fly.

Did You Hear That?

Some of the raptors are thought to have been as clever as a parrot. Do we know how well parrots can think? Obviously, they ask and answer questions, but is this a trick that some trainer has taught them or do they really understand what they are saying? If you or any of your friends have talking birds, you could try to teach them some new words.

We may always wonder if the dinosaurs could talk. Do you think T. rex roared like a lion? Maybe the sauropods made a trumpeting noise with their trunks like an elephant. From their names, what kind of sounds do you think these dinosaurs would have made: Drinker, Gigantosaurus, Hyaenodon, Lambeosaurus, and Pachycephalosaur? Can you and your friends make some of these sounds?

Why did the silly dinosaur wear a baseball mitt?

He wanted to catch a bus!

Chapter 10

Gone But Not Forgotten

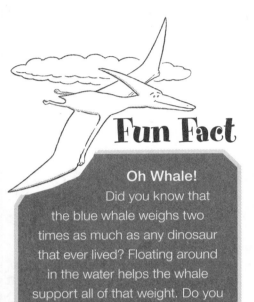

Fun Fact

Oh Whale!

Did you know that the blue whale weighs two times as much as any dinosaur that ever lived? Floating around in the water helps the whale support all of that weight. Do you feel lighter in the water?

Who am I?

By my name you might think that I spent all day long gulping down water. In fact I wasn't any thirstier than the rest of the dinosaurs.

Who am I?

Drinker

Take a Dinosaur Home

When you go to a toy store, what do you see? More often than not, there are dinosaurs peeking at you from every wall, every shelf, and sometimes even hanging from the ceiling. They are one of the most favorite toys of children and grownups. You may have had one when you were a baby, or maybe you have one now that travels with you whenever you go on trips. You might collect them or have stuffed animal dinosaurs on your bed.

Every day, people read dinosaur books, go to movies about dinosaurs, or watch television shows about them. Dinosaurs seem to be almost everywhere, even in the comic strips! Do we like them because we want to be a little afraid of something that we know can't hurt us? How can something that should be such a scary beast be loved so much? For some reason, we are fascinated by them.

Learn All You Can

Most children, as they grow older, want to know everything about the dinosaurs. There are always "how," "when," and "why" questions about the dinosaurs and their past. Dinosaur fads come and go, in some form or another, but each new generation seems to feel the same way about these gigantic, amazing beasts. You could make your own record of what you've learned by creating a dinosaur book or album. Maybe your book will be a sticker book, or maybe it will be a scrapbook made from pictures or posters. Not only are there pictures and books to learn from; some people have made dinosaur statues as large as the real dinosaurs used to be. You could add copies of photographs or drawings of these statues to your scrapbook. If you were able to travel all over the world, you could see them for yourself!

It's easy to make your own statue by using wire, boxes, duct tape, glue, and paper. Your statue could be as big or as small as you want. For some variety, you could make your dinosaur glow in the dark or become fluorescent by coating it with paint you can buy at your local craft store. You could also add scales by using sequins or large circles. Maybe you can create a new kind of dinosaur.

Dinos in Space?

Do you think that the dinosaurs came from the ocean, or do you believe that they might have come from other planets all those millions of years ago? Some of the earliest creatures might have been born on Earth, but were the larger animals a new life form from outer space? Some of the dinosaurs do resemble aliens, or at least something out of this world. Maybe these travelers came at different times or from different places. If other creatures had learned more about space travel, maybe that would explain the incredible variety of dinosaurs that appeared in the Cretaceous period! Some of the dinosaurs died over the years, leaving fossils behind, but who knows—maybe 65 million years ago, the rest of them gave up on this noisy, smoky, constantly moving planet and moved their colonies to another galaxy.

If the dinosaurs came from another planet, will they come again, or will we find them when we decide to journey through the solar system? For some reason, someone decided to take the skull from a fossil skeleton of Coelophysis, whose remains were found all over Pangaea, on the space shuttle *Endeavor,* in 1998. Did those

Fun Fact

Straight Up
Some people wonder if the reason they have problems with their backs might be because some animals originally walked on all four feet instead of walking upright. Do you think the dinosaurs had backaches?

Try This

Surrounded by Stars

You can bring the constellations into your room by using a dark piece of paper. First, punch holes in it to show your favorite group of stars. When you are through, tape the paper to your window so the only light that shines into your room comes from the holes. Or you can purchase glow-in-the-dark stars and planets and stick them onto your ceiling.

scientists believe that Coelophysis should travel in space again? If so, was this why this special honor was given to this dinosaur? What do you think? Can you find the answer?

You can make observations about space with a sky-watching kit of your own. In your kit, you will probably want a map that shows the locations of the most well-known constellations, a small telescope if you can borrow one from someone, a flashlight, and a pad and pencil to write down all that you see. Another way to see the stars is to visit a planetarium.

Dinosaur DNA

What makes you look the way that you do? Each of your parents is responsible, to a certain degree, for the color of your hair and your eyes and the fact that you are a certain height, but sometimes children don't look like their parents or their siblings; they look like their great-great grandparents instead. This is because the "blueprints" that say what you will look like are made of pieces that are passed down from generation to generation.

Carpenters use what they call a blueprint to construct a house. The blueprint shows the final plan for what the house will look like—it tells how big the house will be, where all the windows and doors will go, and so on. Our bodies' blueprint is our deoxyribonucleic acid, also known as DNA, and it is a combination of genetic information from all of our ancestors.

All animals, including the dinosaurs, have DNA. Science-fiction writers have predicted that

Time for Tyrannosaurs

Unscramble the words in the word box. Fit them into the proper spaces to complete each of the following riddles:

1. What do you get if you cross a dinosaur with a wizard?

   Tyrannosaurus _____

2. What happens when you cross a dinosaur with a chicken?

   Tyrannosaurus _____

3. What do you get when dinosaurs crash their cars?

   Tyrannosaurus _____

4. What do you call a dinosaur in a cowboy hat and boots?

   Tyrannosaurus _____

5. How do dinosaurs pay their bills?

   With Tyrannosaurus _____

6. Where do dinosaurs wear their ties?

   Around their Tyrannosaurus _____

7. What does a nearsighted dinosaur wear?

   Tyrannosaurus _____

XHE	XTE	ECKSWR
ECKSCH		CKSPE
CKSNE		ECSSP

Words to Know

amber:
Amber comes from fossilized tree resin. Over time, this sticky substance becomes as hard as a rock. Some of this amber was formed during the time of the dinosaurs.

Try This

Amber Suckers

Would you like to see how amber might look? Coat a saucer with cooking spray and put a piece of butterscotch candy in the center. Fill a cup with water and place it in the microwave oven beside the saucer. Have an adult cook it for 2½ minutes or until the butterscotch melts. Add sprinkle candies and a Popsicle stick, and let it cool before eating!

someday a scientist will find a way to obtain some dinosaur DNA, perhaps from some body part trapped in **amber.** Someday they may even reproduce a T. rex! Some scientists believe that the amber that oozed out of the conifers (cone-bearing trees, such as pines) captured insects. Who knows? Maybe insects, some of which looked like fleas, could have bitten the dinosaurs, and then some of the insects' blood could contain some of the dinosaurs' DNA. If this blood was preserved for all this time, could that DNA still be used?

If they could bring back a dinosaur from a sample of its DNA, would you want one of your own? Maybe you would if they could make a miniature one, preferably with no claws and, especially, no teeth!

Man Versus Evolution

Are we changing our world? Some pet owners prefer small animals because the people live in small homes, or they want a pet that will eat less or not be as frightening to their guests. Over the years, many breeds of dogs have been miniaturized, including the miniature schnauzers and the teacup poodles. Has this changed these animals' DNA? Would these animals grow larger again through evolution if there were no interference from people? The answer may lie in studying wild animals.

In the age of the reptile-like mammals, there were large members of the cat family; they disappeared and then returned as small mammals. Many millions of years later, there were saber-toothed tigers that vanished with the mammoths. We have all sizes of cats in our modern-day world. Will evolution ever change them from four-footed animals to two-footed creatures? Can you imagine what it would be like to see a cat that walked on two feet?

The Return of the Dinosaur

If it were possible to bring back the dinosaurs, should we? Could they hold the key to a cure for many of our diseases, as we hope might be the case for the plants and creatures that we are collecting from the rain forests for research? Would we choose only the small dinosaurs for our experiments? Just like the cats, the dinosaurs started out as very small animals and then some of them became enormous.

Good News or Bad News?

The story about Pandora's box is an old fable about being too curious. It tells about the bad things that can happen if

Who am I?

You might think from my name that I looked sort of icky. Actually, I was one of the most beautiful of the dinosaurs. Some thought that I looked like a moth or a butterfly.

Who am I?

Icarosaurus

Ha Ha

Look at these six pictures. Number them in order so that the story makes sense.

Which One?

Not only would you think that I could come in handy if you were trying to make a sweater; I could have washed it in the river and dried it on my one horn. Which one am I?

A. Goffs Pocket Gopher
B. Woolly Rhinoceros
C. Eastern Elk
D. Stag-Moose

B. Woolly Rhinoceros

What dinosaur coughs the most?

The bronchitis!

you open a tempting box without knowing for sure whether it is filled with treasures or sorrows. Bringing back the dinosaurs could be like opening Pandora's box—no one knows exactly what would happen. What if those small dinosaurs evolved and had a population explosion as they did millions of years ago? Once our planet was filled with dinosaurs, how would we control them?

Try writing a story about how you think your life might be if this could happen. It might be called "The Dinosaur That Lived with Me" or "Living with the Dinosaurs." Try to imagine what it would be like if you were trying to cross the street with a T. rex close by, or if you think the dinosaurs could be trained so they could be used as tow trucks or hook-and-ladder trucks to help fight fires and rescue people. Where would they live and how would we transport them? What kind of world would we have with these new and improved dinosaurs in it?

The Race to the End

If the dinosaurs could be brought back in some way, would they survive? Would there be enough room and food for all of us? We can't even take care of some of the species that we have, such as the elephants, tigers, rhinoceros, pandas, and even the Komodo dragons. Some animal lovers have worked very hard to bring the buffalo, the condor, the bald eagle, and the whooping crane back from the brink of extinction. The list of animals lost to extinction includes many more than those mentioned in this book.

Some of the animals once listed as extinct, such as the fish called the Coelacanth, have been discovered in some remote areas of the ocean or world. Could there be other animals that were believed to be extinct that are really still around?

What Is As Big As a Dinosaur But Weighs Nothing?

Its shadow, of course! Can you find the shadow pattern that matches this picture?

Try This

In the Shadow of the Dinosaurs

One way to picture the dinosaur's world is by making a diorama or shadowbox. You can make your dinosaurs by drawing them. Then cut them out, remove the bottom of the shoebox, place the box on its side and then tape them standing up on the bottom of the box. Set your box in front of a light or window.

Some people have described the dinosaurs as failures, but they ruled the world for millions of years. They were here on Earth close to a hundred million times as long as mankind has been. There were reptiles before the dinosaurs. After the dinosaurs disappeared, these reptiles survived and continued to evolve. Their world changed. Today our world is changing with the loss of our rain forests, swamps, and our clean atmosphere. Will we evolve, or do we need to work on improving our world?

How do dinosaurs apologize?

They say, "I'm dino-saury!"

Fun Fact

Disastrous

Some of the most complete dinosaur fossils ever found were created as the result of a catastrophe. Some of the catastrophes were volcanoes, sandstorms, or floods that buried the animals and kept the air from getting to them, so their bodies didn't decay.

Appendix A: Glossary

adapted
When something changes to fit its surroundings or environment, we say it has adapted. The dinosaurs changed and adapted for millions of years before they vanished.

amber
Amber comes from fossilized tree resin. Over time, this sticky substance becomes as hard as a rock. Some of this amber was formed during the time of the dinosaurs.

amphibian
An amphibian is an animal that lays its eggs in the water. Most amphibians, like the frogs, can live both on land and in the water. Amphibians are cold-blooded animals that have a backbone and rubbery skin.

ancestors
Ancestors are the people or animals in a family that were born before this generation. You descended from your grandparents and great-grandparents, so they would be your ancestors. The dinosaurs were ancestors of the modern-day reptiles.

archosaur
Archosaur means "ruling reptile." Dinosaurs were members of this group of reptiles, which also included pterosaurs and crocodiles. Crocodiles are the only members of the archosaur family that are still living today.

carnivorous
When an animal is carnivorous, it means that he likes to eat meat or the flesh of other animals. Several of the dinosaurs were carnivores, including Tyrannosaurus rex.

climate
The climate of an area is a description of what the weather is like there. The climate that the dinosaurs lived in changed from place to place and from year to year. Sometimes the climate was hot and dry; other times it was wet and cold.

cretaceous
The word cretaceous means having chalk or chalk-like qualities. During the cretaceous time of the dinosaurs, the land was filled with rocks made of chalk or limestone.

descendants
Your parent's descendants are their children (including you!) and their children's families. You are a descendant of your grandparents and parents. The dinosaurs also had descendants that they gave birth to.

excavate
When you excavate something, you remove it from somewhere. The dinosaurs' bones are usually excavated from the ground. Sometimes they are found under the water or layers of rock.

expedition
When the first dinosaur hunters went to search for dinosaur bones they called the hunt or journey an expedition. Some expeditions still take place every year.

extinct
When an animal becomes extinct, it no longer exists or lives on our planet anymore. Dinosaurs, along with many other animals, have become extinct or have vanished from our planet. Some animals are considered endangered, which means they are at risk of becoming extinct.

fossils
Fossils are formed when the remains of a plant or animal become surrounded with sedimentary rock that hardens, leaving an image of the plant or animal that once was there.

geologist
A geologist is someone who works in the field of geology, which is another word for the study of the earth. Many geologists study rocks and the history of our planet.

impression
An impression is a mark or print left behind on something by an object or animal that was there before. Fossil tracks, like those of the dinosaurs, are one type of impression.

Jurassic

Many rocks discovered in the area of the Jura Mountains, between Switzerland and France, were from an era long in the past. Scientists chose the name Jurassic to indicate the period of time those rocks come from.

meteorite

A meteorite is a part of a meteor from outer space that enters the earth's atmosphere. Several meteorites have hit the planet. Some people believe that a meteorite caused the extinction of the dinosaurs.

museum

A museum is a place where different things are stored and displayed for others to see and study.

omnivorous

Omnivorous animals like to eat both plants and meat. Most humans are omnivorous and so were many of the dinosaurs. The Oviraptor was an omnivorous dinosaur.

paleontologist

A paleontologist is someone who examines or studies fossils, like those of the dinosaurs. Paleontologists work in the scientific field called paleontology.

Pangaea

Pangaea is the name given to the lands of the earth at the time when they came together to form one continent millions of years ago. The name Pangaea means "all earth." Scientists have found clues from fossils that show that the dinosaurs existed at this time.

prey

When one animal hunts another animal, the animal that is being hunted is called the prey. Many of the smaller dinosaurs were prey to the larger meat-eating dinosaurs.

pterosaurs

Pterosaurs were bird-like reptiles that flew through the air during the time of the dinosaurs. Some of these pterosaurs had wings that spanned up to 40 feet across.

reconstruct

When you reconstruct something, you rebuild it. When the fossil hunters find the many broken pieces of dinosaurs they take them to museums, where workers put them back together or reconstruct them.

reptile

A reptile is a cold-blooded animal that usually lays eggs and has a backbone. Most reptiles have a scaly or tough skin. The dinosaurs that lived millions of years ago were reptiles. Snakes, lizards, crocodiles, and turtles are a few other reptiles.

science fiction

When people dream or write about what could be in the world of science, they call it science fiction. A long time ago, the thought of bringing dinosaurs back to life was considered science fiction. Now it could be closer to reality.

specimens

Specimens are samples of something. If you wanted to know how a batch of cookies turned out, you could sample one; that cookie would be a specimen. Dinosaur bones are specimens that teach about dinosaurs.

survivor

A survivor is one who succeeds in lasting a long time. The dinosaurs survived for millions of years on an ever-changing planet.

theory

Many scientists have theories or ideas about the way that the dinosaurs used to live. When we are unsure about something we are left with theories or guesses.

Triassic

The word Triassic comes from the word tri, which means "three." There were three types of rock that were common during this time of the dinosaurs: sandstone, mudstone, and shale. Scientists now refer to this particular time period as Triassic.

Appendix B: Do Your Own Research

Web Sites About Dinosaurs

www.bear-tracker.com
See tracks and photos of reptiles, amphibians, and mammals.

www.brainpop.com
Visit the science section of this site and experience all kinds of dinosaur fun and activities.

www.dinodictionary.com
Here's the site for pronunciation of all of those dinosaur names. It also gives the meaning of the dinosaurs' names.

www.dinosaurpark.org
A place where you can see Dinosaur Park's exhibits and take a virtual tour of its museum.

www.dino-web.com
This site includes virtual dinosaur games, information, and a place to vote for your favorite dinosaur.

www.enchantedlearning.com
Enjoy dinosaur games, info, jokes, crafts, and quizzes.

www.ology.amnh.org
A fun-filled site with activities, trivia, drawing tips, dinosaur skeletons, and more.

http://rockhoundingar.com
This site contains almost everything a beginning rock collector should know.

Books About Dinosaurs

Cam Jansen and the Mystery of the Dinosaur Bones (Cam Jansen Adventure)
by David A. Adler (Author)
Publisher: Penguin Putnam Books for Young Readers; Reissue edition

Dinosaur Detectives
(The Magic School Bus Science Chapter Book #9)
by Judith Bauer Stamper (Author)
Publisher: Scholastic

Dinosaur Encyclopedia
by David Lambert (Author)
Publisher: Dorling Kindersley Publishing; 1st edition

Dinosaurs! : The Biggest Baddest Strangest Fastest
by Howard Zimmerman (Author)
Publisher: Atheneum

Dinosaurs Before Dark (Magic Tree House #1)
by Mary Pope Osborne (Author)
Publisher: Random House Books for Young Readers

Eyewitness: Dinosaur
by David Norman (Author)
Publisher: Dorling Kindersley Publishing; 1st edition

How to Keep Dinosaurs
by Robert Mash (Author)
Publisher: Weidenfeld & Nicholson; Rev. updated edition

National Geographic Dinosaurs
(For the Junior Rockhound)
by Paul M. Barrett (Editor)
Publisher: National Geographic

Outside and Inside Dinosaurs
by Sandra Markle (Author)
Publisher: Aladdin; 1 Aladdin edition

What Happened to the Dinosaurs?
(Let's-Read-and-Find-Out Science 2)
by Franklyn M. Branley (Author)
Publisher: HarperTrophy; Reprint edition

page 4 • What?

1F	2C	3E	4F	5D	6B	7F	8C			9E	10E	11F
A	N	Y	T	H	I	N	G			Y	O	U

12A	13C	14A	15A		16A	17C		18D	19B	20B		21D
W	A	N	T	–	I	T		C	A	N	'	T

		22C	23D	24D	25B		26C	27E	28C	
		H	E	A	R		Y	O	U	!

A. Being identical
T W I N
15 12 16 14

B. Water from the sky
R A I N
25 19 6 20

C. Behaving badly
N A U G H T Y
2 13 28 8 22 17 26

D. To not play by the rules
C H E A T
18 5 23 24 21

E. Round toy that goes up and down on a string
Y O Y O
3 27 9 10

F. Popular fish in a can
T U N A
4 11 7 1

page 9 • If At First . . .

TBRNBY
BTRBYN
TNRYNC
EBRBAN
TONPBS

TRY-TRY-TRY-CERATOPS

page 10 • Fossil Fractions

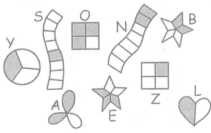

L A Z Y   B O N E S
½ ⅔ ¼ ⅓   ⅖ ¾ 2/7 ⅗ ⅛

page 17 • Shell Game

page 20 • Chop It Up

W	H	A	T	'	S		T	H	E		B	E	S	T	
W	A	Y		T	O		T	A	L	K		T	O		A
	L	I	O	P	L	E	U	R	O	D	O	N	?		
	L	O	N	G		D	I	S	T	A	N	C	E	!	

page 25 • There, There, It's OK

CHEER
HIM
UP!

PUZZLE ANSWERS

page 30 • Ptiny Pterosaurs

page 35 • Prehistoric Protection

Is it true that a Velociraptor won't attack if you are carrying a tree branch?

That depends on how fast you carry it!

page 37 • Raptor Rebus

When can three Velociraptors get under an umbrella and not get wet?

When it's not raining!

Where was the Velociraptor when the sun went down?

In the dark!

page 43 • Full Plates

What do you call a dinosaur who makes noise as he sleeps?

STEGOSNORUS

page 44 • Heads or Tails

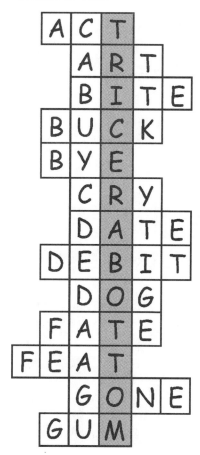

A	C	T		
	A	R	T	
	B	I	T	E
B	U	C	K	
B	Y	E		
	C	R	Y	
	D	A	T	E
D	E	B	I	T
	D	O	G	
F	A	T	E	
F	E	A	T	
	G	O	N	E
G	U	M		

133

page 50 • Puzzle Master

page 58 • Dino-mite!

Dino <u>score</u>

Dino <u>bore</u>

Dino <u>sore</u>

Dino <u>shore</u>

Dino <u>store</u>

Tricera <u>cops</u>

Tricera <u>hops</u>

page 60 • What Is Noisier Than a Hadrosaurus?

page 63 • Curious Question

Question:

Why are there only old dinosaur bones in the museum?

_____

Answer:
Because they can't afford to buy new ones!

page 63 • Fierce Fossil

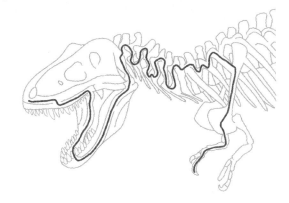

page 71 • How Do Scientists Know That Some Dinosaurs Were Professional Racers?

T B G B H J G J E B J G M Y B G J F B J B O
J U M B J X N J M J D M B X X F M X M X O M
B M S X S G X B I B M M L J G M I G Z J G J
M G M J X J B M M B G X J M G M X J X B M E
D X G M D G X G J I M B M N X J B X O X J X
B M S X B X A M M X U M J M R X X M J T X G
J X G J M J M M B G X J J B X G J R M X B M
B G M J A X G X C X J K X G M J B X B M J S

They found fossilized dinosaur tracks!

PUZZLE ANSWERS

page 73 • Find the Fossil

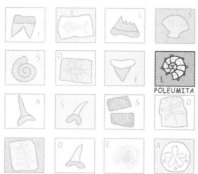

A petrified Tyrannosaurus
is "A COLOSSAL FOSSIL!"

page 78 • Dino Discovery

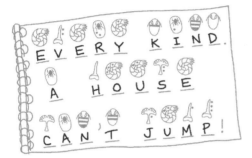

EVERY KIND.
A HOUSE
CAN'T JUMP!

page 84 • Keep Looking

page 87 • Flying Fossil

page 93 • Why Don't Dinosaurs Ever Forget?

Because no one ever
tells them anything!

PUZZLE ANSWERS

page 98 • **Prehistoric Pairs**

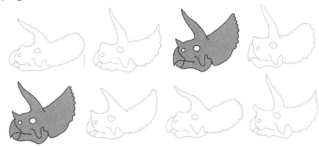

page 100 • **Why Did the Dinosaur Cross the**

Because chickens had
not evolved yet!

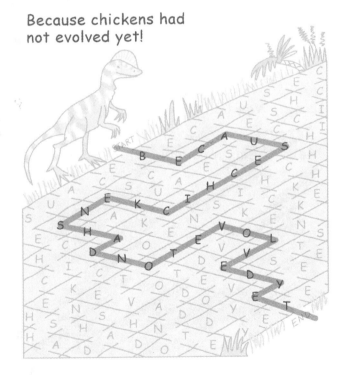

page 105 • **End of the Story**

THEIR TAILS!

page 111 • **Space Traveler**

Toothosaur   alien   Tankopod   Sailosaur   Flipodon

page 114 • **Gotcha!**

	I		D			
	N	I	R	U	S	L
B	E	I	E	A	A	E
A	B	C	A	W	R	S	Y
B	E	C	A	U	S	E
	I	T		W	A	S
A	N		E	A	R	L	Y
	B	I	R	D	!	

136

page 117 • What Did One Fossil Say to the Other?

Oh, not much changes for me!

A. Move like a dog's tail
W A G
1 25 26

B. An opening to let out air or water
V E N T
12 17 19 4

C. A place to live
H O U S E
2 21 22 28 27

D. Past tense of eat
A T E
11 15 7

E. To move gently back and forth
S W A Y
5 8 3 20

F. Number after eight
N I N E
14 23 24 13

G. To reflect light
S H I N E
16 10 9 6 18

page 123 • Time for Tyrannosaurs

1. What do you get if you cross a dinosaur with a wizard?
Tyrannosaurus hex

2. What happens when you cross a dinosaur with a chicken?
Tyrannosaurus pecks

3. What do you get when dinosaurs crash their cars?
Tyrannosaurus wrecks

4. What do you call a dinosaur in a cowboy hat and boots?
Tyrannosaurus Tex

5. How do dinosaurs pay their bills?
With Tyrannosaurus checks

6. Where do dinosaurs wear their ties?
Around their Tyrannosaurus necks

7. What does a nearsighted dinosaur wear?
Tyrannosaurus specs

page 125 • Ha Ha

page 127 • What Is As Big As a Dinosaur, But Weighs Nothing?

The Everything® Kids' Series

All New GROSS Series

The Everything® Kids'
Crazy Puzzles Book
1-59337-361-9

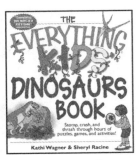

The Everything® Kids'
Dinosaurs Book
1-59337-360-0

The Everything® Kids'
Gross Jokes Book
1-59337-448-8

The Everything® Kids'
Gross Puzzle
& Activity Book
1-59337-447-X

The Everything® Kids' Backlist

The Everything® Kids' Animal Puzzle & Activity Book
1-59337-305-8

The Everything® Kids' Baseball Book, 3rd Ed.
1-59337-070-9

The Everything® Kids' Bible Trivia Book
1-59337-031-8

The Everything® Kids' Bugs Book
1-58062-892-3

The Everything® Kids' Christmas Puzzle &
Activity Book
1-58062-965-2

The Everything® Kids' Cookbook
1-58062-658-0

The Everything® Kids' Halloween Puzzle &
Activity Book
1-58062-959-8

The Everything® Kids' Hidden Pictures Book
1-59337-128-4

The Everything® Kids' Joke Book
1-58062-686-6

The Everything® Kids' Knock Knock Book
1-59337-127-6

The Everything® Kids' Math Puzzles Book
1-58062-773-0

The Everything® Kids' Mazes Book
1-58062-558-4

The Everything® Kids' Money Book
1-58062-685-8

The Everything® Kids' Nature Book
1-58062-684-X

The Everything® Kids' Puzzle Book
1-58062-687-4

The Everything® Kids' Riddles &
Brain Teasers Book
1-59337-036-9

The Everything® Kids' Science Experiments Book
1-58062-557-6

The Everything® Kids' Sharks Book
1-59337-304-X

The Everything® Kids' Soccer Book
1-58062-642-4

The Everything® Kids' Travel Activity Book
1-58062-641-6